Fact and Fiction About Phonics

Fact
and Fiction
About
Phonics

Roma Gans

Illustrated by Tom Funk

33884

The Bobbs-Merrill Company, Inc.
A Subsidiary of Howard W. Sams & Co., Inc.
Publishers • Indianapolis • New York • Kansas City

Foreword

The teaching of phonics has suddenly awakened wide interest and general questioning. Parents, professional educators, and other citizens have become involved in the topic and even, at times, quite stirred up over their differences of opinion.

As in dealing with most aspects of education, individuals express strong feelings and firmly held opinions but reveal little information about phonics. They should not be blamed for this last shortcoming, because materials relevant to the teaching of phonics have not been assembled in one handy reference.

To help interested persons, the most important aspects of the subject are presented in this publication. It is hoped that the information included on phonics in the English language, young children's learning in phonics, the various opinions on phonics, and the suggestions for introducing phonics in reading and spelling not only will quiet some of the anxieties but will also benefit the learning of children.

West Redding, Connecticut　　　　　　　　　　　*Roma Gans*
November 5, 1963

Contents

1. How phonics reached the limelight

In an age marked by breathtaking inventions in space, bone-chilling threats of war, and heart-warming achievements in medicine, one must ask how such an undramatic topic as phonics caught the eye and ear of Mr. Everyman.

At a recent conference assessing topics of domestic interest for their universality, tax revision, the "population explosion," states' rights, and water pollution were named and calmly commented upon. Then problems and issues of education were named, and the word *phonics* was mentioned. A sudden burst of interest and strong feeling broke forth. The chairman, genuinely surprised, asked, "Why this emotional concern over phonics?"

Yes, why does the very word *phonics* evoke heat? A cursory inquiry might reveal that many who are excited about phonics may not even be able to provide a more precise definition of the word than "It has something to do with learning to pronounce words." True, the use of phonics does have "something to do" with learning to pronounce words. More than that, the use of phonics is absolutely essential not only to a beginner in reading but also to adult readers. When we encounter a word new to us, such as *electronics,* we tap the phonic resources that we acquired in our first years at school. We "think" the sounds, syllable after syllable, as we read silently. Yet we are scarcely aware that we are pausing in our reading, and we certainly do not stop to reflect that "now I must use my phonics."

Most of our reading is done by means of automatic responses acquired through much reading, even when we meet the complicated non-phonic spelling patterns of words like *ought* and *school*. Charles C. Fries aptly describes our reading when he states: "The major spelling patterns of present-day English are fortunately few in number, but for these the reader must develop, through long practice, high-speed recognition responses. These responses must become so habitual that practically all the clues that stimulate them eventually sink below the threshold of attention leaving only the accumulative comprehension of the meaning."[1]

A child, less experienced, might sound out the word *electronics* but still be quite conscious of the specific phonic learnings he is using in pronouncing it. However, both experienced adult reader and beginner must call upon phonics to translate the letters into sounds in order to pronounce the word. Without phonics, we would have to rely solely on sight recognitions and memory of each word. A new or unlearned word would slow us down or completely stymie us. Phonics is an essential collection of elements that everyone must master if he is to develop competence in reading.

Some causes for the excitement

Most of us were taught phonics step by step in the primary grades in school, but, as with much of our early schooling, we may recall very little of it with any degree of reliability. Some of us may honestly report, "I don't remember ever being taught phonics or even being taught how to read." The use of our knowledge in phonics is so completely assimilated in the total

---

[1] Charles C. Fries, *Linguistics and Reading*. New York: Holt, Rinehart and Winston, Inc., 1962, 1963, p. xvi.

intellectual process of reading that we are seldom conscious of using it. Indeed, we cannot remember ever having learned anything about it.

Some youngsters arrive almost at that high point of proficiency in third grade, and the very keen may become "phonics wise" even earlier. The majority of youngsters can read with ease and fluency with the aid of proper use of phonics before they leave the sixth grade. Not all. Among the few who struggle year after year to sound out words, who require much adult help, and who often grow to dislike reading are those who, even with able tutoring, cannot seem to catch on to phonics. Parental concern over such stragglers has ignited some of the furor over phonics. But not all the excitement can be laid at the door of worried parents. Others, less legitimately concerned, have seized on this anxiety as an opportunity for personal gain. Much of today's undue stress on whether children are being taught phonics, or how well or "correctly" this is being done, has been generated and kept alive by such "worry-mongers." Most of the concern, legitimate and less so, is centered on the beginning-reading period. This is reasonable, because the use of phonics is noticeable in the beginners' reading.

Some questions about methods used in teaching beginning reading over the past several decades are quite proper. A brief look into the trends in the teaching of reading will shed light for those who have entered the education profession recently, who have not followed this phase of education closely, or who are perplexed over the fuss and stir about phonics.

A brief look at past emphases in teaching reading

During World War I, standardized tests of intelligence, the Army Alpha and the Army Beta, made their debut. Although studies regarding the improvement of testing methods were going on, the use of tests to measure the intelligence of groups caught the imagination of psychologists and educators. Many of them were ready to develop new frontiers in measuring both native ability and achievement of school-age youngsters. Appropriately, the entire field of reading came in for an avalanche of research: speed of reading; eye span; and grade-level achievement. Correlations of reading achievement with a variety of factors were among the many studies undertaken. Some findings exerted a great influence upon the teaching of reading. One of these was the finding that excessive use of oral reading correlated highly with a slow rate of silent reading.

The reading-with-expression era. At that time, respect for competence in oral reading was still deeply rooted in the minds of educators and lay people. Competence in reading was commonly tested by having a youngster read orally. He was judged as a good reader not only by his fluency, but also by his "expression," his inflections, yes, and even his posture.

Today's critics cite evidence of a lack of ability to apply

phonics; at the turn of this century, similar critics harped on the poor quality of oral reading. Elocution was highly regarded. So important was the matter of reading with expression that the following advice was offered to teachers in the front pages of the *Second Reader of the School and Family Series:*

We begin at the outset, in "the Primer," to teach correct reading, by giving numerous examples, in nearly every lesson, of the various kinds of easy and natural questions and answers; thus exercising pupils in reading, *with the proper inflections, the very sentences they are constantly* speaking.[2]

---

[2] Written by Marcius Willson and published by Harper & Brothers, New York, in 1886.

In the section following, titled *"Inflections,"* examples of questions and answers were given, and to be sure the teacher understood, several examples were printed as follows:

                                        ly?
                                dent-
        Did he act pru-
                        e?
                m
            o
        Has he c

                                        day,
        Has he gone to town to-   or will he
            m
    go to-   o
            r-
                r
                o
                w?

A large variety of materials and instructions was given to teachers to eradicate the criticism that "Schools are not teaching oral reading adequately." Parents who could afford to do so saw to it that their children took lessons in elocution. Undoubtedly, some parents felt that the school was remiss because such private tutoring was necessary. As might be expected, minimal attention was paid to speed in silent reading. But then, this was before the age of speedup.

Excessive labialization or sounding of letters. A natural accompaniment of what was considered good oral reading was the clear pronunciation of each word. Phonics, a recognized element of reading, was also emphasized. To be sure that a child acquired a distinct manner of reading, phonic elements were exaggerated, or labialized, when pronounced: *ch*air, *c a p, sh*all, and *m o* re.

Excessive use of lips, tongue, and breath gave the oral reading of young readers a slow, staccato, and explosive quality. Such emphasis added to the slowing down of the reading process.

Emphasis on speed emerges. With the advent of tests that could measure many aspects of reading and the subsequent high regard for statistical studies, a large number of "discoveries" about the status of reading was made. The rate of silent-reading speed from very slow to very fast was clocked. The correlation of speed with oral reading was computed. Testers reached the conclusion that fast silent readers read with a minimum of vocalization and slow readers tended to vocalize noticeably.

Following the reports of such research findings, a program of re-education of school personnel and revision of the education of prospective teachers got under way. As a result, with the enthusiasm we characteristically display in the United States, silent reading became *the* first concern, and oral reading was not only given limited time, but was even forbidden in some schools. The emphasis on oral reading with expression was replaced by a stress on silent reading to improve speed.

Uncertainty about phonics sprouts. Anyone acquainted with school practices could notice a minimizing of the excessive use of vocal apparatus in blurting out beginnings of words and certain syllables. The time formerly consumed daily by one child reading while all the others listened was now used for work in silent reading. In first-grade classrooms, the time allotted to teaching phonics and other word-study exercises was markedly reduced. Much of the time saved was used for work with flash cards and exercises in phrasing or grouping words.

These last exercises were intended to improve the functioning of the child's eyes in reading. Fries makes an interesting observation regarding this particular concern: "In spite of the great number of studies dealing with eye movements (or better, "eye-pauses"), very little of a positive nature has been contributed to our understanding of reading ability and to our knowledge of how to develop it in either children or adults."[3] The purpose of such effort was to increase a child's "eye span" and thereby increase his reading speed. Children were advised to read "by taking eyefuls" rather than word by word. Such emphases were given high priority at teachers' meetings, at state and national conferences, and in the professional literature. During this period, if a barometer on regard for phonics could have been created, it would doubtless have registered a falling esteem for

---

[3] *Linguistics and Reading,* pp. 30–31.

phonics as a word-recognition technique and a sudden rise in regard for the speed of reading per se.

Phonics, still recognized as an essential element in reading, soon came under another scrutiny. New reading systems were developed. These included instructions to teachers to develop increased competence in see-and-say word-recognition techniques, rather than sound-out-and-say, which was the former phonic approach. Although the teaching of phonics was not discarded, it was so minimized that teachers became uncertain about its desirability. They were also instructed to prevent labialization and to reduce vocalization. In silent reading, there was to be "no use of speech organs and no sound."

Between 1920 and 1930, the uneasiness regarding the teaching of phonics became so widespread that a book by a prominent reading specialist, Dr. Arthur I. Gates, written for school administrators, included the chapter "Phonics or No Phonics?"[4] Dr. Gates was one of the early authorities in the field of reading research who recognized phonics as an essential tool but who offered help to teachers in developing other techniques of recognizing words—by sight or total configuration, cues, and structural analysis.

Common instructions to teachers on phonics. The two most common sources of instruction to teachers at that period of shifting emphasis were the methods classes in normal schools and teachers colleges and the manuals that accompanied basal school reading books. From these, teachers received such instructions as the following:

1. Start teaching phonics after the child has acquired a sight vocabulary of approximately sixty words.

2. Give each child an opportunity to read silently every day.

---

[4] Arthur I. Gates, *Reading for Public School Administrators*. New York: Bureau of Publications, Teachers College, Columbia University, 1931, p. 126.

3. Reduce oral drill and use silent-reading practice material instead.

4. Keep children from moving lips or reading audibly in silent reading.

An informal group of supervisors, deeply concerned with improving instruction in reading so as to increase speed and silent-reading comprehension, reported—in a class at Teachers College, Columbia University—in 1929 that not one school of the many visited had *eliminated the teaching of phonics*. They also reported that teachers showed great uneasiness and that some complained about the insufficiency of material on teaching phonics in their teacher-preparation methods courses.

Uncertainty about drill arises. To cause further distress to teachers—and to youngsters who were affected by the teachers' confusion—another new theory was emerging. This, the project method, was to affect the entire education program. William H. Kilpatrick, noted educator at Teachers College, Columbia, was the key innovator of this method. Kilpatrick was greatly influenced by John Dewey's analysis of learning through experience. Kilpatrick, who always kept his teaching close to classroom practice, translated the more esoteric ideas of Dewey into everyday language to help teachers see their implications for teaching.

In general, the project method included the following characteristics:

1. A topic or problem important to the children was selected for study. Such topics as "Our local water supply system" and "How granite is quarried" might be selected.

2. The children shared in planning the work to be done in the study.

3. All subjects, such as history, science, geography, and skills in reading, writing, and arithmetic, were called upon as needed for the study.

4. The particular type of reading skill and all other learnings

essential to the study formed the basis for further practice and drill.

5. The children shared in planning a summation and in evaluating the work and testing the results. Those phases of the work which had value for further studies and for later reviews were recorded.

6. The time devoted to a project often required daily periods of several hours per day for weeks and even months.

In addition to the project, the regular class program included the subjects, skills, and arts not included or adequately developed in the large study. Nevertheless, *the main work* of the day was that related to the project, and as much learning as possible was an integral part of it.

The interest generated by the project method stirred both enthusiastic adherents and acid critics. The principal criticism was that skills, notably reading and arithmetic, were neglected and that children were spending too much time on lesser learnings, such as art, construction work, and discussion. To answer such criticism, Ellsworth Collings[5] conducted an experiment in three schools in Missouri. He gathered data on the measurable achievement of children in a project-centered curriculum, comparing children in this program with children of equal ability taught in separate-subject programs. Tests were given at the beginning of the experiment (1917) and again four years later.

According to a study of the results, the forty children from the experimental school achieved more than did the forty pupils with whom they were paired. The ten skills and subjects measured were (1) penmanship quality, (2) written composition, (3) spelling accuracy, (4) American history information, (5) geographical information, (6) reading comprehension, (7) addition accuracy, (8) multiplication accuracy, (9) subtraction accuracy, and (10) division accuracy. In addition to this successful achieve-

---

[5] Ellsworth Collings, *An Experiment with a Project Curriculum.* New York: The Macmillan Company, 1923, Chapter 4.

ment, the experimental school had less absence, tardiness, and truancy than did the other, and more of its students than of the other school's completed the eighth grade and continued into high school.

Intelligent use of the method. As is so often the case, an educational theory has intelligent accepters and half-baked followers. The intelligent teachers saw the additional values offered by the project method. First, children became motivated and so identified with the work that they not only accomplished more, but they also entered fields of learning previously considered too difficult for them. Second, they saw the sense in what they were doing; it was not "I must do this work for the teacher," but rather, "I need to get this for my work." Third, much of the significance of their learning became apparent in relation to its bearing upon other phases of study. For example, the youngsters studying their local water-supply system saw maps of underground pipes. Map-making, formerly considered only in relation to geography, was now seen to be essential to certain civics problems. The measurement of the capacity of tanks was now recognized as essential application of mathematics to planning for a daily living need.

Rather than, as formerly, emphasizing learning skills in order "to be good at them," children came to respect skills in terms of their importance to their work; instead of learning facts in history and geography for examination purposes, they came to respect fact-acquisition as an aid in understanding problems and issues. This was the learning encouraged by wise teachers and intelligent school leadership.

Misinterpretations and common errors. Not so in all classrooms. Some teachers—and so-called school leaders—snatched up single elements or symbols of the project method. "In order to do projects you've got to have a workbench," said a teacher who

was rationalizing a narrow program of 3 R's emphasizing memorization at the expense of thinking and of helping youngsters to see the meaning of what they "recited." In another situation, every teacher was required to have an elaborate assembly program following the conclusion of a project. The teaching tended to focus on the assembly, and the youngsters learned very little.

A very common mistaken interpretation of the project method, responsible for ludicrous teaching and serious omissions, was the idea that *all* learning had to be tied in with the project. Arithmetic, geography, spelling, English, history, music, and even health were in some way to be studied as integral aspects of a project—no matter what the particular project happened to be.

Such absurd teaching offered critics a rich field of examples of quackery in teaching. One of the most amusing of these criticisms, written by Allan Abbott, was entitled *A Fish-Centered School.*[7]

A careful look at what happened to all skills and particularly to reading in this epoch in curriculum history is relevant here. Teachers with inadequate or no guidance and those with the tendency to jump on bandwagons, sans professional understanding, did neglect children's need for direct teaching of reading techniques. They also failed to provide many children with time and proper materials for drill or practice. The careful day-after-day work on guiding beginners to recognize words by their general characteristics, commonly called *word configuration,* or by applying phonics was either totally neglected or at best allotted inadequate time. Sufficient practice for those who needed much repetition to be sure they remembered was also neglected. As a result, some children whose teachers were given to loping rapidly over learning experiences failed to learn to read in primary grades. The majority, however, mastered the skills and profited—in spite of poor teaching.

Concern over methods of teaching reading. Parents whose seven- and eight-year-olds were not progressing in reading quite naturally joined the critics in attacking new methods. Charges of displacing the 3 R's with fads and frills, failing to teach children the fundamentals, and, that worst of all accusations, "being too progressive," were common. Because this was the period of greatest activity and influence of the Progressive Education Association, many separate criticisms were ultimately lodged under one banner, that of "anti-Progressive education."[8]

---

[7] Allan Abbott, *A Fish-Centered School and Other Educational Whimsies.* New York: Bureau of Publications, Teachers College, Columbia University, 1936.

[8] Lawrence A. Cremin, *The Transformation of the School, Progressivism in American Education, 1876–1957.* New York: Alfred A. Knopf, 1961.

Great strides were made in increasing the quality of comprehension in reading, in developing the skills required in reference reading, and in inspiring thousands of youngsters to become selective, intelligent readers who pursued their reading voluntarily; but these achievements were overlooked.

School systems across the country conducted testing programs to show uneasy communities that the 3 R's were not being neglected. Rapidly mounting data revealed that children *were* being taught to read in the so-called progressive programs, and that their reading was better than that measured under similar circumstances with similar tests twenty-five and more years earlier. To reasonable inquiries into the schools' work, such investigations were reassuring. Unfortunately, too many, once aroused, overlooked the evidence: "Don't bother me with the figures, I know."

What! No phonics? The uneasy climate that prevailed in the 1930's calmed down during the World War II period. Concern over family members in the service, the daily absorption in food rationing, and other essential adjustments drained off much interest and energy. The schools were beset with a great variety of problems, among them absorbing the children of migrant families, getting along with minimum supplies, and keeping a semblance of adequate teaching personnel.

However, once the war was over and communities, all zooming with growth, began to re-establish "business as usual," the attacks on the schools were resumed. But now the attacks had a new focus—the failure to teach phonics. The field for this attack had been fertilized in the preceding decades with criticisms, both reasonable and unfounded. Now, in days of crowded schools, anxieties over the burgeoning space age, and ever increasing financial pressures, more enrichment was added to the soil. A new wave, "let's-get-back-to-phonics," washed over us.

Later on, in separate chapters, these attacks and the counterproposals for teaching will be described. At this point, it is enough to recall several facts: The teaching of reading over the years has been a handy target. Shifts in teaching emphasis caused uneasiness among teachers as well as parents. A lack of intelligent regard for phonics was discernible after major efforts had put an end to slow, meaningless, wordy oral reading. Unwise or misguided teaching did result in a loss of learning, especially for some not-so-eager youngsters. And, in times of stress, otherwise sensible parents and lay citizens can be influenced by opportunists who prey upon their anxieties.

Other factors contributed to present worries over learning to read and over the early use of phonics. One important point, however, is all too often inconspicuous. The specific nature of the English language is a major consideration in this phonics tempest in the educational teapot. A look at our language is so important to anyone interested in the field of phonics that the next chapter is devoted to it.

2. Some facts about the un-streamlined English language

Most of us first learned how to use English from hearing members of our family speak it. Certain sounds that made up words were conveyed to us with such clarity and in such meaningful contexts that we, in turn, could use them in conveying our ideas to others.

To those accustomed to our language, "it sounds simple." Most of us grew into its use unaware of its multilingual history. But a noted linguist, Mario Pei, points out: "Persian and English have borrowed half their vocabularies from foreign sources."[1] A child says *garage* with accustomed accent, not realizing that he is using a word borrowed from the French. He refers to a *dachshund*, unaware that he is using a German name. He may call attention to a *hydrofoil* skimming over the water, without ever being aware that there is such a language as Greek, from which the prefix *hydro* can be borrowed. Such common words as *ought* have descended from early English, and their

---

[1] Mario Pei, *The Story of Language*. Philadelphia: J. B. Lippincott Company, 1949, p. 129.

spelling still plagues youngsters in learning to read and spell, but not in learning to use them orally.

Experienced listeners actually hear only 50 per cent of all sounds. We become so adept that we listen literally with "half an ear" because we can piece out the rest without listening. By the time a normal five-year-old comes to kindergarten, he, too, is able to listen with this hear-and-piece-out quality. This is a very important point to remember when we attempt to understand the child's first approach to phonics.

First contacts with phonics

In learning to read, a child meets a more complicated function of language than he does in learning to speak. In reading, he comes upon symbols called letters, arranged in sequence in words that represent meanings. To get at the meaning, he must be able to translate the letters into sounds, so that he can identify the words they stand for. When he sees the word *free,* he must translate the letters into an *fr* and *ee* sound, then blend them and sound out *free.* When he does this, he is using phonics. Phonics is the term commonly used for the process of translating individual letters and combinations of letters into sounds that identify the word they represent. In oral reading, the word is pronounced; in silent reading, it is heard in inner intellectual recesses. If a child recognizes the word *free* from some previous experience without sounding it out, we say he has learned it "by sight." Through either phonics or sight, he eventually recognizes the word with ease and ultimately with the seeming "unawareness" that adult readers reveal. By looking at word after word after word, a child grows in the speedy recognition of words.

Danger—it seems so simple. The foregoing description, stripped of many of its real qualities, is accurate, but it is far from complete. Yet this is the way in which many adults have come to regard the complicated process of learning to apply phonics. The following account seems appropriate here. One evening, at a parent-teacher meeting in Long Island, the teachers of the primary grades described the variety of techniques and materials they used in teaching reading. One parent, apparently disturbed over the slow progress his seven-year-old son was making, asked: "Why all that to-do about teaching kids to read when the main business is to get them to pronounce the words? All you have to do is to give them the rules for pronunciation, then see that they apply them."

Would that it were that simple! For German, Spanish, and Italian, heavy reliance upon rules is more appropriate, because these languages have more consistency in the relation of sound with letters. Not so with English, the language we are interested in exploring, particularly as it affects a child's efforts to learn to read.

Two fields are pertinent in gaining a more adequate understanding of the child's acquisition of phonics as an aid to his reading. The first is the nature of phonics as inherent in written English, and the second, the way in which a young child tends to learn. The casual observer needs a degree of understanding of both in order to avoid oversimplification or quackery.

An examination of only some of the irregularities, inconsistencies, and complexities found in the spelling-to-sound relationship in English words follows. Its purpose is to help us recognize the burden carried by a young child in first sounding out words. A complete phonetic or linguistic analysis of English words would make up a comprehensive volume. The vignette presented here, however, will highlight the problem faced by a child in his first contacts with printed English words and will help us to be more realistic and understanding about his frustrations and bewilderment. It will also—it is hoped—challenge the soundness of the theorists who believe that an all-phonic approach to beginning reading should be the Heaven-sent manna for all children.

A look at vowels—their regularity and vagaries

Our alphabet of twenty-six letters is made up of five vowels, *a, e, i, o, u* (and *y* when it is sounded like *i*), and nineteen consonants. The vowels are produced in an easy, flowing manner, without the nearly explosive or forceful pressure required in sounding consonants such as *b, d,* and *p*. Vowel-sound effects are subtle to the young listener's ear. Indeed, some of the variations are too subtle for most adult ears to detect. Only phoneticians and others experienced in speech have such competence. Many dictionaries, for example, ascribe eight variations to the sound of *a*, from *ā* as in *cāke* to *a* as in *sofȧ*. Some linguists have analyzed the language and have discovered more than forty sounds of *a*.

The standard sounds of vowels vary according to their use in words. Knowing when *a* sounds *ä* or *ă* or *ā*, or is silent as in *tēar*, presents a problem that those deeply concerned with the teaching of phonics should pause to examine. The rules are neither few nor simple.

One of the most regular sound-symbol rules which a child acquires in his reading career is that a vowel is usually long,[2] or says its name, when it occurs in a short one-syllable word that ends in a silent *e*. Such words as *cake, pole,* and *bike* are con-

---

[2] *Long* and *short* are used in this work to indicate the ā, ă, ē, ě, etc., sounds.

sistent with this rule. To understand it, a youngster must have learned previously that a syllable is a collection of letters that blend into one sound—like *ate, be,* and *ing.* He will also need to feel at home with the idea of one-syllable and two-or-more-syllable words. In addition, he must have acquired the auditory acuity to hear the *ā* sound as distinguished from other sounds. Children with hearing problems commonly reveal their handicap in their efforts to identify vowel sounds.

One rule for short vowels, though apparently simple, also requires specific learnings: A vowel is usually short when it is in a short word or syllable ending with a consonant, such as *făt* and *bĭtten.* The short words will obviously be easier for the child to manage than the two-syllable words. He may quickly notice that *fat* is a short word ending in *t*, which is a consonant; therefore, the *a* sounds ă. The word *bitten* places a heavier burden on him, because he must be aware of the proper place to divide the word into two syllables: *bit* and *ten*. Teachers and reading specialists commonly defer work on methods of syllabification until children are beyond the beginning-reading period, even though the children frequently meet words to which this rule applies. However, the rules regarding when vowels are long and when short might be considered "merely the beginning."

Enter the vowel digraphs. In many common words in the English language, two or more vowels are used together. They often present a real stumbling block to both child and teacher, because those that are exceptions to the rule are almost as common as those that fit the rule. One general rule is that when two vowels are together, the first is given the long sound and the second is silent. Words like *tāil* and *bēat* fit the rule, but everyday words like *does* and *hour* do not. Some exceptions are so frequent that rules for them have been created. (Many of us still recall at times the spelling aid "*I* before *e* except after *c* or when sounded as *a* as in *neighbor* and *weigh*." In some words, the first vowel is short and the second, silent, as in *health* and *weather*. Vowels are also influenced when used with certain consonants, especially *r*. The *i* in *girl,* the *o* in *work,* and the *e* in *her* take on special sounds that are neither long nor short.

The sound of vowels is affected also by the point at which the accent falls in a word. As a rule, in a two-syllable word, the vowel in the accented syllable is long. The one in the other syllable is given the slight or indistinct sound called *schwa,* as in *brōken, hīking,* and *dāred*—but not always. Words like *water* and *began* do not follow this pronunciation principle.

The intention here is not to present the rules that govern the sounds of vowels used singly or in combinations in words.

Instead, this brief examination of vowels is intended to remind those of us who recognize words automatically of the problem vowels present to a child learning to read English through an "all-phonic" approach.

Consonants

Consonants are simpler to pronounce than vowels are. To begin with, most consonants demand more physical action in being sounded than do the vowels. Children can actually feel themselves pronounce *b, m, z,* and *d*—especially at the beginnings and ends of words. Most consonants are fairly consistent in their sounds, and, therefore, to the child they seem more "reliable" than vowels. However, one consonant, *c,* is particularly fickle. In certain uses, *c* takes on the soft sound of *s;* in others, the hard sound of *k.* A child often starts to pronounce such words as *cent, city,* and *certain* with the hard sound of *k,* as in *care, car,* and *come.*

Some consonants must seem like useless additions to words, not only because they are silent but also because it would be almost impossible to pronounce them in the words if they were not silent. It must seem to a reasonable child that such words as *ought, catch,* and *gnome* are foolishly spelled. Nimble children enjoy exploding the *b* at the end of *dumb,* the *h* in ghost, and the *k* in *knew.* No wonder people of far less note than George Bernard Shaw have argued for a revision of spelling in order to remove some of the gross dislocations between symbols and their respective sounds.

Consonant blends and digraphs. Although consonants do present less variation of sound, and therefore fewer complications, to the young reader, the nature of the sounding-out difficulty they cause should not be glossed over. Notice the variety of consonant blends in a short list of everyday words:

*br*ead	*dr*ive	*gr*ew	*sk*in	*sp*ell
*bl*ew	*fl*ew	*pl*ace	*sl*ip	*st*ir
*cl*ear	*fr*ee	*pr*ize	*sm*og	*sw*at
*cr*ab	*gl*ad	*sc*at	*sn*ore	*scr*eam

Each blend has its own sound effect. A child may understand the sound of *b* in *big* and *r* in *ray* but struggle to sound *br* in *bread*. So with every consonant blend. Each demands of the child its distinctive sound.

When two consonants are used in pairs known as digraphs, they may cause a more serious stumbling block to the child than consonant blends do. In the blends, the letters maintain a semblance of their characteristic sound when their sounds are smoothed together. In consonant digraphs, neither letter keeps its sound identity. The following words illustrate this fact of phonics:

*ph*oto	*wh*ere	*sh*all	*ch*eap	*th*e
*ph*onics	*wh*y	*sh*e	*ch*air	*th*is

No wonder Dick, who was a poor speller, included words such as these in a list he titled "Phoolisch werds."

There are many more cases in which sounds deviate from normal expectations, especially to a beginner or a less experienced reader—or to a child not versatile in the English language. Imagine the amount of explanation needed to give the reasons underlying pronunciation of *one, son, sun, upon, no, not,* and *on.* These examples are high on word lists used in books for beginners. If their recognition and oral pronunciation were to be taught solely via phonics, pity the teacher and the children.

And still more: syllabification and accent

Early in a child's reading career, he meets the word *syllable,* which, according to definition, means "those letters in a word that, when taken together, make one sound." Words of two or more syllables are readily spoken by children—and some are also quickly recognized in print. *Christmas, Halloween,* and *birthday* are commonly recognized and clearly pronounced by children even before they have heard the word *syllable.* They notice that some words are long and are pronounced sound after sound. However, the rules for syllabification are commonly deferred until after the third grade.

Many young readers acquire considerable awareness of syllables through their discovery of common suffixes. One class of first-graders changed the simple jingle "I can ring, I can sing, I can swing," to "I am ringing, I am singing, I am swinging." Following the discovery that they could add the suffix *ing* to these three words, they extended the list to include *playing, eating, sleeping,* and *working.*

The suffix *ed* would not lend itself to such easy discovery as did *ing. I can play* could be changed to *I played,* but *I can eat* would be followed by *I ate.* The high frequency of irregular verbs adds to the complexity of learning correct English usage. No wonder that many who acquire English as a second language find it difficult. A teacher who is aware of the irregular qualities in our English language is quick to sense when children's explorations will lead to the discovery of a general pattern or rule and when they may highlight irregular forms and word structures.

Children, for example, can understand suffixes and can see

the function of word endings such as *ing, ed,* and *es.* However, in their early attempts to use them, especially in spelling, they quickly meet a variety of regulations and exceptions. "I did pay for my milk," wrote Gerald to his teacher. "'Yes he payed it," wrote Cynthia, who was the class bookkeeper. Rules for when to drop the final *e* and when to double the final consonant before adding a suffix cannot usually be acquired until the children become mature enough to assimilate such regulations. However, before that time, they can learn to be ready for the unexpected. This is particularly true when they write and must spell. For this reason, some points regarding phonics and spelling are included in the last chapter of this book.

In sounding out polysyllabic words, one must learn where to place the accent if the word is to be pronounced acceptably. This aspect of phonics is usually relegated to older children, those old enough to use a dictionary. This is reasonable. A child is often in a quandary about where to place the accent or stress when he meets a word in reading that he does not commonly hear or use. One rule—namely, that in two-syllable words, the accent is usually on the first syllable—can be understood by the younger readers. Emphasis on this seems unnecessary, however; most of the words a child recognizes in his reading convey to him the pronunciation to which he is accustomed. It is when his reading vocabulary begins to extend beyond his listening vocabulary that the pronunciation of new words may require a knowledge of rules and of accent placement, and the use of a dictionary.

Word meaning and pronunciation

Some words we call *homonyms* take their pronunciation from their meaning in the sentence. The word *tear* in the sentences "I shall *tear* the paper along this line" and "I saw a *tear* roll down his cheek" are examples of this added irregularity. A thoughtful reader who, when reading orally, pronounces *read* as *rĕd* instead of *rēad* discovers his error. The relatively large number of homonyms occurring in the child's everyday writing call for special attention in teaching spelling. Here, spelling in relation to meaning must be acquired. When a child asks, "How do you spell *here*?" an alert adult asks, "How are you using it?" or says, "Tell me what you wish to write."

Whose pronunciation is correct? Anyone who travels in the United States and who listens attentively will notice pronunciation characteristics indigenous to particular areas. He will hear a man discuss his *"idear"* in Maine and his *īdē* in southern Missouri. He will meet far more *äh* sounds in the South than in the Dakotas, and he will surely notice the slighting of *g* by North Carolinians describing their *"workin', runnin',* and *playin'."* Many of these geographical speech characteristics are accepted. Some, however, like the *dis* for *this* and *ting* for *thing* stemming from the German influence in some Midwestern sections, are not accepted. In general, however, phoneticians and linguists are tolerant about the liberties taken in pronunciation. Proof of such tolerance can be found in any dictionary that includes several pronunciations for a large number of words.

When Junior asks, "What's this word?" The foregoing brief account of the irregularities of vowels and consonants, of vowel digraphs and consonant digraphs, of silent and schwa sounds should at least alert us to the nature of the problem that faces beginning readers and their teachers. When a child asks, "What's this word?" an adult informed in the variation of letter sounds will not say, "Sound out the letters." Instead, a helpful parent might say "Spell it out, if you know all the letters. Then I can tell you what the word is." In the beginning period, many youngsters can read before they know all the letters. With them, when they ask for help, it is best to say, "Show me the word."

We have examined some of the irregularities in the pronunciation and spelling of our language. It is equally important, however, that we pause to consider the young child and the abilities he summons in learning to read this inconsistent language. The next chapter will be devoted to some facts about young readers.

3. Some facts about children

When and how to teach phonics are questions directly concerned with the initial reading period; therefore, they include implicit assumptions about the ways in which young children can and should learn. We adults may be quite aware of the manner in which we approach something to be learned, and we may have memories, sometimes reliable and sometimes fancied, of the way in which we learned in our early childhood. What we may not fully appreciate is that the understanding of young children and the ways in which they learn have been and continue to be the subject of a tremendous amount of significant research. Informed teachers and school leaders are, therefore, not applying outmoded practices, nor are they pulling their methods out of fanciful hats. Instead, like true professionals, they are basing policies and practices on what is known about children's learning.

The assumption that children are like adults, only smaller, younger, and less experienced, has long since been discarded. The assumption that they learn as adults do has been debunked too. Unfortunately, it still persists in much adult thinking. Later on, in an examination of the various theories of teaching phonics, evidence of some mistaken ideas on this point will be presented. The reason for these errors can be briefly stated: In many instances, those who understand the ways in which young children work do not seem to understand the complexities of phonics, and often those who understand phonics do not understand how young children can best be guided to learn.

A veteran teacher, for example, unschooled in such details of our language as are included in the previous chapter, may not be sufficiently aware of the reason why a first-grader is unable to sound out the first word of a story he is trying to read. The word is *once*, one of those highly irregular words. Such a teacher needs a basic review of her understanding of English words in order to revive the acuteness she may previously have had. An energetic young salesman of a phonics system who tells a group of alert teachers, "Don't let children point out words or letters in signs they see, they need to get letters and words taught in the proper sequence," is burdened by the assumption that children will submit to blinders and then, like an adult, follow the content, step by step, as taught. An energetic young child cannot and should not be so controlled or manipulated.

Children—"no two alike"

Although we readily agree that children are unique and differ widely, even within the same family, we often act as if we do not believe it. In one instance, we are pleased to notice how a child in whom we are interested stands out as a unique personality; in another instance, we may be quick to ask why he differs at this point. "I would never confuse your Ellen with any other girl in kindergarten," said a teacher to a mother, who seemed pleased to hear this. When the teacher commented that Ellen seemed more shy than the rest of the group, however, the mother was less pleased. True, we want a child to have all the acceptable attributes, but we also want him to be sufficiently unlike other children to be recognized as a unique individual.

Thank God for this desire. It counteracts, in part, the tendency to pressure children toward uniformity that is observed all around us, in homes, schools, churches, and community organizations. It seems to be a quality indigenous to American life today.

In writing on the significance of being unique, Earl C. Kelly, a specialist in the psychology of human behavior, raises the question, "Considering the biological basis for uniqueness and the obvious advantages of it to the individual, how can we account for the fact that our culture is so antagonistic to it and does so much to reduce and, if it were possible, to destroy it?"[1]

In referring to schools (not all), he states: "The basic pattern of the schools in general is to ignore the individual and to level out the differences between people. . . . It is frowned upon

---

[1] Earl C. Kelly, in *Our Language and Our World,* ed. S. I. Hayakawa. New York: Harper & Brothers, 1959, p. 160.

when a learner, through curiosity, knows something which is ahead of the lesson taught. . . . The standardized "lesson" requires that learners be alike."[2]

In contrast to such tendencies, there are two strong influences, in addition to individual inheritance, that work upon children and create the wide differences so noticeable among them. The first is the environment into which they are born—that is, the type of immediate-family and neighborhood life in which they spend their first five or six years. The second is the intellectual vitality they bring to the many opportunities they meet, minute by minute and day by day. Obviously, these two are related: The nature of the child's world affects to a degree the way in which he acts and reacts in it; and the intellectual strength, only a part of it inherited, with which he meets experiences in his world helps shape its effect upon him. The continuous give-and-take between the child and his everyday living helps shape his uniquenesses, his strengths, his shortages, and his distinctive qualities.

The major importance of environmental influences, although an established fact, still is not widely known and certainly is not commonly acted upon. We are indebted largely to the work of the French researcher, Jean Piaget, for his penetrating studies of children, starting in the 1920's. In summarizing the oustanding work of Piaget, J. McV. Hunt calls to our attention one of Piaget's conclusions pertinent here, namely, that Piaget's observations and experiments indicate that a child's ways of behaving and thinking are continually changing as a result of environmental influences.[3]

This major insight is still quite frequently ignored or refuted by such common statements as "He has a high IQ" or "She is

---

[2] *Ibid.,* p. 162.

[3] J. McV. Hunt, *Intelligence and Experience.* New York: The Ronald Press Company, 1961, p. 246.

not college material." In other words, the labeling of children as bright, dull, and often "ready for reading" or "unready," implies an acceptance of the now discarded concept of static intelligence. In contrast, the emphasis on understanding the background and contemporary environment of a youngster and the effort to present each child with a wide, rich array of interesting and challenging opportunities in school is in harmony with the latest promising understanding of a child's potentially changing intelligence. Teachers and all who are interested in, and work with, children must delve into backgrounds and accumulated experiences so that they may understand a child and his uniqueness. Upon the knowledge gained, they may build further experiences that will nourish the child's continued growth.

The child's environment

One facet, and an important one, of the total environment of a child is the language he hears and starts to acquire. If you are concerned with the way in which a particular child may use phonics in learning to read, it would be sensible to examine carefully the language background of the child. If your concern with phonics is more general, however, try to understand the variety of language influences to be found among the children in one contemporary classroom.

The child's early experiences with sounds. In learning to sound out the words that he sees before him in a book, a child must draw upon his auditory acuity and his previous listening experiences. The very language he speaks he has acquired by capturing sounds through his ears. The teacher who is alert to evidences of children's hearing reflects respect for an essential

physical power in learning. Schools that insist upon an early and competent audiometer test of each child reveal proper concern for a child's general well-being and essential fitness for learning. Children with hearing deficiencies, even minor ones, have difficulty in hearing certain letters, such as *h*, and whole words, even when they are close to the person speaking.

The amount and variety of experiences with sounds that a child gains through listening to radio and television and to people speaking around him contribute to the "experienced ear" he brings to kindergarten. Some children live in families that enjoy conversation. Such children can "tune in" to many voices and speech variations. They have had many personal conversations with adults and with other children. Some of the speech they have heard may have been clear because words were pronounced distinctly, and they, too, may use a relatively distinct articulation. Others may have been surrounded by careless speakers, and they may speak carelessly or be less articulate. Nevertheless, from a variety of sounds, a young child's ears have become experienced in hearing.

By the time he is five, through this daily live-and-learn existence, a child has also collected a vocabulary of from two thousand to more than five thousand words. He understands them when they are used by others and can use them himself in correct context. Some of the more agile learners have vocabularies of far beyond five thousand words.

In addition to language experiences, many children acquire a great deal of auditory education through music, heard over radio, television, and recording machines, and in family playing and singing. It is not uncommon in a kindergarten to hear some children sing on pitch, reveal acquaintance with a large repertoire of music, and indicate marked ability in "intelligent" listening to music. Those who have had such privileged experiences obviously can readily hear the differences between words such as *her* and *were*.

Unfortunately, not all children come from a family with the time, talent, respect for children, and resources to provide this type of rich background. Some families live in a rather silent way, with little conversation, communicating largely by gestures and monosyllabic comments. Their life may be devoid of music. Children from such families will reflect such limitations. They may have had little conversation with parents or any other adults. Similar limits may be shown when parents have work schedules that prevent frequent contacts with their children. Older children may play the role of guardian for these children during parents' working hours. Children in large institutions, too, often suffer from lack of opportunity for conversational relationships with adults.

Another observation about young children bears repeating here. It is common for them, even when they have good language backgrounds, to confuse words or run them together, not appreciating where words begin and end. This is understandable. When we adults listen to a language strange to us, we, too, fail to appreciate which sounds make individual words and which are a part of longer words. A kindergarten teacher, aware that children may sometimes hear a collection of sounds as a "glob," played a game with them. She would say a short sentence or phrase—"Come here," "I can see you," and so forth—and ask the children to tell how many words she had spoken. Then she asked the children to speak and tell how many words they used. Ginny, an eager responder, said "Whatchagot?" The teacher asked, "How many words, Ginny?" "One," she exclaimed.

The child's growth as an acute listener and accurate reproducer is closely linked with his beginning work as a reader. To expect him to "tune in" quickly to the specific sounds of words and parts of words without reference to his hearing experience is unreasonable. It may put him at such a disadvantage as a beginning reader that he is seriously discouraged. The clarity with which he speaks is of equal importance. A child's acquired way of speaking also affects his reading. In referring to the articulation of young children, Dorothea McCarthy, a child psychologist who has studied the speech development of young children, states: " . . . the child with faulty articulation usually has faulty perception of speech sounds, or faulty motor responses in attempting to make speech sounds, and the resultant model which he furnishes for himself to imitate is imperfect so that he continues to practice error."[4]

Preschool acquaintance with books. Youngsters with good preschool care who come from a family in which books are cherished and read to children have also gathered some important learnings related to phonics. Such children notice letters and

---

[4] Dorothea McCarthy, in *Manual of Child Psychology,* ed. Leonard Carmichael. New York: Wiley and Sons, 1946, p. 544.

the use of signs and are aware of the function of reading in life around them. Some can actually *read* signs, their own names, and a number of words that they have encountered under circumstances that particularly impressed them. Interestingly enough, many of the words they learn in preschool experiences are identified by configuration, or the "looks of the word," such as *Halloween* and *giraffe*. Some words are recognized by cues—the letters *Ch* at the beginning may indicate to a child that a long word is *Christmas*.

Such self-teaching by the child counters one of the points at issue, which will be described in the following chapter. Certain theorists charge the schools with thwarting or hampering children's reading by teaching them to recognize words at sight or by configuration or context cue. It seems as if children answer these critics by saying, "Try and stop me." Only if we blindfold children or remove all print from their view can we stop such word recognition by sight or cue. School, for many such youngsters, is not the place where they are "introduced" to symbols but,  rather, the place where they continue to grow in the power of translating symbols, letters, and numerical figures into their proper meanings. An informed kindergarten teacher suggests to children early in the fall that they bring their own favorite books from home. The result is heartening. Today, many children from homes that might be described as "unliterary" have books of their own. Even specific learnings in beginning the art of reading—once assumed to be the function of the school—children acquire from parents, relatives, community contacts, and bookstands in the shopping centers.

The variations in experiences with sound that their environments have offered are, to a large degree, responsible for the variations we find in children entering school. Informed teachers and school leaders know this and plan accordingly. Such professional educators will also remember that the sounds that we utter per se are not the significant elements of language, but the meanings that they convey are. The words the child reads orally and pronounces distinctly are not the important achievement of reading; rather, it is the meaning that these words convey to him. This idea needs to be called to our attention frequently and also to the child's, lest in our concern over a child's progress in becoming a reader we lose the richness of reading through our overemphasis on the mechanics of word recognition and pronunciation.

Individual learning power

Some children seem to have built-in self-starters. They are aggressive about exploring, discovering, and "wiggling" or manipulating their world. Others are less so. The reasons for this difference are many. One primary influencing factor is parental guidance. Some youngsters are helped and encouraged to be self-sufficient. They live in a home atmosphere that frees them to look about, to inquire, and to learn, even at the expense of some mistakes and inconveniences. Others are kept dutifully quiet, clean, and less aggressive. Even with encouragement, however, some remain shy, uneasy, and slow-growing in the ability to reach out and add to their awareness and understanding of what goes on about them.

Some of the difficulties are owing to the makeup of the child. In other words, innate ability or inheritance does have some effect, but a child is assured a greater chance to extend his intellectual powers if we stress the importance of rich give-and-take living for him.

The child will express his power through seeing, hearing, touching, asking, listening, experimenting, playing, imitating, and in all the other ways in which he is busy from morning until bedtime. A home and immediate neighborhood furnished with equipment, toys, and a variety of other materials, in which a child, preferably with other children, can lead an active, interested life, is a power-building influence. Add to such a stimulating situation cheerful, patient, and intellectually responsive adults who talk with and listen to children, and the children will increase those abilities and strengths which we commonly refer to as "intelligence."

Children's methods of learning

Anyone who takes time to observe a three-, four-, or five-year-old for one day from sunup until his bedtime will be impressed with the wide array of information he already has assimilated and the skills he can call into use. He demonstrates by what he does and says how much he knows about his surroundings. "I need to borrow my Dad's wrench to fix my bike." "My mother never lets me work her mixer." "You don't dare open the mail. Only my mother does that." "They are drilling a deep, deep well in our yard so we'll get lots of water—then I can make a swimming pool." Not all three-year-olds have such language facility, but many do. They reflect the way in which they are included in life about them, the things that are happening nearby which have been explained to them, and the information they are acquiring under safe, wholesome living conditions. The old phrase "They absorb so much" is indeed true.

Catching on by absorbing. Some further consideration of the manner in which they absorb and assimilate so quickly, apparently with ease, is very important at this point. Much of what they learn is unplanned for them—instead, it "happens" about them. Much that is going on may be ignored. What they react to may vary and may often be hard to predict. Vigorous motion— the flurry of a passing fire truck or the loud, scraping sound of a steam shovel—can be relied on to arrest their attention. We cannot know, however, whether they will stop in their play to listen to a record being played or to watch birds bathing in a shallow pool. Nevertheless, of one thing we can be sure: The more interesting and varied the experiences they do share in, the more their knowledge will expand, and the larger their meaningful vocabulary will become. A young child grows in acquiring language through his daily contacts with interesting activities. Such growth is highly important to his later success in reading.

Some key points about qualities young children reveal in learning need to be kept in mind, especially in an effort to evaluate phonic programs.

We are constantly surprised when young children reveal some new-found skill or piece of information. We have frequently heard the question, "Now where did he learn that?" Children seem to snatch things out of the air and, in a seemingly effortless way, "latch onto" new words, new mannerisms, and new skills. Most of us recall an instance of their embarrassing skill in eavesdropping and remembering.

The amount of learning in preschool years with this snatch-and-run rapidity and ease should make us pause and reflect on a single feature of the child's methods of learning: Without a *lesson* or *tutoring* or *step-by-step* structured experience, he amasses an amazing understanding of the world about him— about people and what they eat, how they dress, and what work they do; and about the fixity or variability of routines. The idea that children "begin to learn once they get to school" is sheer nonsense. In an unstructured non-lesson way, they learn from birth on. The amount and desirability of what they learn depends largely upon the conditioning influences of their immediate home-community world. A preschool background rich in experiences for a child to "live up" will stretch his powers. Yes, his IQ.

Caution! Don't hold them back. A preschool background meager in experiences or one that prohibits a child from reaching out and exploring will lessen his powers and may even hamper his ability for life. Research studies,[5] chiefly with animals, on sensory deprivation in the early periods of life are consistent in their findings; first, the early period of life is the foundation-building period for later power; and second, deprivation in the early period may produce irreversible effects. Similar experiments with children, of course, are not possible; but similar conclusions have been drawn from observations of children in environments that limit opportunities.

Specifically how the child intellectualizes during this period has frequently been studied. It is wrong to think that he is putting forth no effort, even if his knowledge seems to accrue in a jovial, almost nonchalant, manner. Were he to be seated and kept at a task of learning even the same elements, he might rebel, show lack of interest, and refuse to learn. For the preschool years and for most young members of kindergarten and first grade, the informal, busy, varied life that is free of step-by-step structuring is best for successful learning. This is another important point to keep in mind when examining specific proposals for teaching phonics to kindergartners and first-graders.

---

[5] Philip Soloman, ed., *Sensory Deprivation—A Symposium Held at Harvard Medical School.* Cambridge: Harvard University Press, 1961.

Flitting while learning. Young children, according to studies, have short interest spans. They may stay at some activity for twenty minutes, or more on occasion; but, as a rule, they move from one interest to another in periods often less than twenty minutes long. But the flitting-from-here-to-there quality does not tell the whole story. They may run from a pile of interesting scrap wood to see what is being whipped up in the blender that has started to whir in the kitchen. Later on, perhaps immediately, or even a day later, they will return to the manipulation of the wood. Their interests do wax and wane, but most do not fade out completely. When young children are allowed leeway to leave and return to ongoing work, this is in harmony with their method of learning. The carefully planned, stick-to-the-job program found in formal nursery schools, kindergartens, and first grades is not. At the age of five and six, some very mature youngsters are ready for more specific planning and more organized activities, but many need the freer, less formal approach.

Searching for reasons. From the age of three, most children begin to notice causal relationships. "What makes it run?" "Why did Mary cry?" and similar questions reveal that they have learned that actions create results. The wider their contacts with their world, the greater the learning in such thinking, and the more frequent the questions for reasons. Children's growth is enhanced if the one of whom the question is asked answers clearly and briefly, but with enough detail to help the child extend his thinking. Youngsters are able to accept rules for their behavior, and they do so more readily if the reason for the regulation is explained to them. They also become sticklers for consistency and constancy of regulations. The "on-and-off," "sometimes yes, sometimes no" in a vacillating family environment bothers them.

Annoyance with variation. Lastly, young children need a feeling of assurance, an I-know-this feeling of power. They need to be on a sure footing on many occasions in a day so that they can stretch to meet the not-yet-known. They show irritation over conflicting weather reports, a shift in planned schedules, and conflicting answers to questions. They want to know *once and for all time.* One child, fascinated with the bright red fire engine at home, could not understand why the fire engine in his grandmother's town was white. "It isn't supposed to be white, all fire engines should be red," he complained several times during his visit.

Part of the young child's eagerness for "facts that stay put" comes from his intellectual immaturity. He needs to grow to generalize properly: "Fire engines usually are red, but I once saw a white one." He needs guidance in and out of school to develop this ability and to learn to allow for exceptions. Even for adults, faulty generalizing is one of the thirteen common errors listed by Stuart Chase in *Guides to Straight Thinking*.[6] It is unfair to young children, then, to expect them to cope with statements that are true at one time and not at another, as: "Plurals are formed by adding *s* or *es* except in such words as *beef, beeves, sheaf* and *sheaves,* etc." Yet some children can and do sprout the ability to generalize accurately. They should stir the adults among us who persist in saying, "I've never yet known a good Smith."

The problem takes shape

A respect for the unique qualities of children, for their eager, learn-as-you-run method of gathering knowledge and skills, for their struggle for reasons, constancy of facts, and dependable information helps us to understand why they respond as they do to some early school experiences. When a child who has found satisfaction in asking "Why?" must face the irregularities and unreasonable qualities of the words he reads, he may experience real frustration. One solemn, serious six-year-old said angrily, "Spelling makes no sense." Young children, properly guided, want things to *make sense*. They have learned that the non-sensible is undesirable before they reach school age. To a reasoning and reasonable child, phonics needs to be presented with respect for this persistent quality.

---

6 Stuart Chase, *Guides to Straight Thinking*. New York: Harper & Brothers, 1956, pp. 39–50.

With proper consideration for the child and his way of approaching learning at the beginning of his school career, and with due respect for the English language, with its multiple sounds for certain letters and combinations of letters, its inconsistencies, and its historic hangovers, we can examine more clearly some of the popular fictions about teaching phonics, presented in the next chapter.

4. Some popular fictions about teaching phonics

It is easy to understand and accept baseball fans and sports-car enthusiasts, but phonics devotees tax one's comprehension. Where else but in the United States could a subject as prosaic as phonics attract sufficient attention to breed self-styled devotees and fans of "brand" systems? There is so much emotionalism associated with the subject that the sweeping generalizations and exaggerated claims for and against systems are to be expected. Yet, it is amazing that some exorbitant and reckless claims have been put in print. The entire matter might be viewed as an entertaining, even amusing, affair were children and parents not included in it.

Scholarly and responsible work has been done and is continuing to be done in the field of phonics. Linguists, including such specialists as Charles Fries, John B. Carroll, and Robert Hall, have opened up to interested teachers and the lay public the complexities of the English language and have offered detailed analyses to help us recognize and understand words in their contexts. They have attempted to enlighten adults on the makeup of our language, not, as a rule, to advise educators how to apply their interpretations. But some exceptions to this gen-

eral rule have appeared—for instance, a book by Leonard Bloomfield and Clarence L. Barnhart, *Let's Read*.[1]

The term *linguistic method of reading,* however, has become
a catch phrase for many approaches to the teaching of reading.
To be in step, a method must not only be "phonetic," but it
must also be "linguistic." One is reminded of the jibes H. G.
Wells enjoyed making about American slogans and our love of
"catchy" titles. He would find a rich field for his sport right
now. To the semanticists who have devoted careful attention
to the meaning of language, however, this wave of language mis-
management must be depressing. Would that each ardent expo-
nent of one theory or system would read—with understanding—
C. K. Ogden's and I. A. Richards' *The Meaning of Meaning*.[2]

Some educators, concerned primarily with the teaching of
reading, have contributed research, helpful analyses, suggestions, and materials for teaching phonics to teachers. Their
work is based upon contacts with the teaching of reading in
classrooms, and upon the type of assistance sought by teachers.
The work of such specialists varies from individual to individual, but each has developed his theory close to the realities of
the classroom and the psychology of learning. Such specialists as
A. Steryl Artley, Emmett Betts, Edward W. Dolch, Arthur I.
Gates, and William Sheldon, commonly associated with the
professional literature on teaching reading, have developed theories and have offered suggestions for teaching phonics, but they
are not to be associated with the panacea peddlers and phonics
pushers. They have their proponents and opponents, but the
atmosphere surrounding them is relatively calm. A contrasting
group of "phonics experts," equipped with other proposals and

---

[1] Leonard Bloomfield and Clarence L. Barnhart, *Let's Read—A Linguistic Approach*. Detroit: Wayne University Press, 1961.
[2] C. K. Ogden and I. A. Richards, *The Meaning of Meaning*. New York: Harcourt, Brace and Company, 1923.

materials, has claimed to offer an inclusive and final answer to every child's beginning-reading needs. These "experts" emphasize teaching a child the phonic elements essential to recognizing words *to the exclusion of other techniques of word recognition.*

The reading specialists among those previously named differ specifically at this point. They include in their theory, along with suggestions for teaching the essential phonic elements, other word-recognition techniques. Their programs for teaching reading, therefore, are not open to the key criticisms lodged against those who advocate an exclusively phonic approach.

Deficiencies in some popular phonics theories

Some phonics programs ardently recommended to teachers, boards of education, school leaders, and parents have raised widespread criticism for a number of reasons. There are some criticisms common to practically all, some to a certain few. Only those points most frequently cited and considered to be serious deviations from sound practice are presented here. Most err in the field of basic understanding of young children and their approaches to learning; others, in a basic understanding of the English language; some, in the widely accepted meaning of the term *reading;* and some, in all these areas.

Erroneous assumptions about young children. The previous chapter has described the uniqueness of the young child's ways of learning in preschool and early school years. Some children learn to recognize letters and words before they enter kindergarten; others, before first grade. Many have a sizable vocabulary that they recognize at sight from early home and neighborhood experiences with books, labels, and signs. Some are keen listeners and observers, with marked auditory acuity. Others, less experienced, may not have developed in noticing or hearing the language about them and may be on the verbal-visual level of three-year-olds. This immaturity may not be a result of inborn lack of ability, but rather of too little social experience in family and immediate neighborhood living. A good school expects this variation among beginners and plans a program rich for each, retarding for none. Obviously, therefore, such schools do not endorse a uniform program in the language arts —in speaking, listening, beginning reading, writing, and the rest.

Error 1. It is precisely at this point that certain phonics programs are challenged. In their advertisements and instructions to teachers, some prescribe materials for *all pupils* of kindergarten or first-grade age; others provide phonograph records with specific phonic sounds, plus rules that are recommended for use in a given sequence or organized "course" *for all.* In such instances, youngsters who are already able to unlock the sounds of words by themselves, and who are ready to sprout through added initiative and responsibility, are discouraged from doing so. Those with limited ear training, who are not yet able to detect differences in sounds, may be dubbed low in intelligence or *unready* for reading.

Uniform "daily doses" or lessons, accepted symbols of the inferior teaching from which few children within a group can profit, are now being returned to many classrooms via *new* phonics courses. To imply that a set of materials, rules, exercises, or films is suitable for all children in a classroom at a given time is sheer fiction.

Error 2. Another erroneous assumption about young children is that the world in which they learn is bounded by the school. One phonics system recommends that the child use only this system's materials in one part of the reading-readiness program. "Be sure to withhold reading in other pre-primers until —— is completed" is the firm instruction given to teachers. One alert teacher asked, "Who thinks this can be done?" Children pursue reading not only in school but outside school as well. Many youngsters have a large collection of library books at home— and primers and pre-primers that older brothers and sisters have passed on to them. One school sent out a letter of caution

to intelligent parents of preschoolers, warning them that children's preschool use of books "might interfere with our new phonics approach." So children's early and eager enjoyment of books may be dampened in order to teach them to read. How fantastic and incongruous.

Error 3. A serious error involving the understanding of young children is the emphasis placed on "giving children the phonics facts" in predigested manner, thereby failing to respect their ability and need to discover and explore. For example, in a good classroom, children experiment eagerly and discover that seeds properly watered sprout better than those not well cared for; that the shadows on the school ground are at a given place in the early morning on a sunny day, but move to another location by noon; that certain words look almost alike, as *some* and *same, lean* and *loan;* that *Helen* and *Ellen* sound very similar; and that *b* at the beginning of a word helps one start sounding out the word *big.*

Error 4. The tightly structural sequence of lessons or the forced daily phonics feeding not only interferes with or prevents full participation in what should be an exciting business of learning for children, but it also demands of them a learning effort for which even some nimble youngsters are not ready. Bruner,[3] in his description of the way in which young children learn, especially if they are to become intuitive and creative thinkers, indicates that their approach to learning is not, for the most part, tightly structured or in orderly steps. They pull fragments or parts of whole ideas from here and there, and gradually their variety of observations takes form. Teaching rules and generali-

---

[3] Jerome S. Bruner, *The Process of Education.* Cambridge: Harvard University Press, 1960, Chapter 2.

zations first, then developing them, conflicts with the way in which youngsters at five and six think.

A student of young children's learning rightfully asks, "Will this tightly planned program administered in daily lessons diminish or weaken the exploratory, creative, and intuitive nature of the child? Will it encourage him to sit and wait to be told how to be dutiful and carry out an assigned task?"

The last two questions are of such importance that those planning school programs that include a formalized step-by-step phonics system should feel responsible for helping to seek answers to them. If we fed children a "patent diet" advertised to boost their strength, we would certainly feel obligated to observe the children's health so that we could note the effects. Furthermore, the proof of the desirability of any given material or method for learning rests upon two tests: What is its immediate effectiveness in meeting the one teaching need for which it is intended? And what is its long-range effect on the child's whole development pattern? For example, the effectiveness of phonics teaching in terms of later interest in reading and depth of comprehension is pertinent in evaluating such teaching. So, too, is evidence that children increase in initiative and responsibility in pursuing their learning, and that they continue to apply their knowledge of phonics not only in reading, but also in spelling.

As children grow from their early stage of learning via first-hand experiences to exploring, guessing, and gradually building insights, they are ready for different, more mature approaches, unless they are intellectually still immature. Phonics work with most children who are in second, third, and later grades, can therefore be systematically planned. At this older age, they are also able to see the connection between an element of a total process and its function in the process. Thus, a child can see the sense of a rule about the various ways of making plurals, because he now is mature enough to write, and he is able to see that the rule makes it possible for him to spell accurately.

A young kindergartner or first-grader may notice and memorize items taught in phonics lessons because he wishes to be a dutiful learner and please the teacher. The relevance of the particular point may be beyond his experience or thinking ability, unless he happens to be one of the very alert and mature, three or four of whom may be found in many classes. In a program geared to fit the ability levels of all the children in the group, these agile learners would get the next steps they are ready for. In the meantime, the other members of the group would continue to enjoy beginnings in reading and would continue to grow in recognition of letters, words, and sounds, according to their intellectual readiness.

All of them would continue to recognize words as they did in preschool years at home, by cues and total configuration. It seems appropriate here to point out again that, despite the emphasis of some phonics specialists, children do use their own powers of observation in the recognition of words. Young four-year-olds can and do acquire considerable accuracy in word recognition by seeing a word and making a connection with its meaning. The mother at a grocery store who said to her four-year-old, Ginger, "Run back to the shelf and get a bottle of apple juice," was not surprised when Ginger returned with the right product. "How did you know?" asked the sales checker. "It says *Apple* here," said Ginger, as she pointed. "She knows the names on lots of boxes and jars because she helps me in the kitchen," explained her mother.

Thousands of preschoolers without a single lesson in phonics acquire a roster of words they recognize, begin to notice some consistency of sound and letters on their own, and develop some independence in reading before entering first grade. These are the nimble learners. While they are acquiring this power, they may not be able to tell how they recognize letters or words. They may not even know the alphabet! A common answer to the observer who asks, "How could you tell this said *Betty?*" might be, "I just can tell," or "I know." Imagine such youngsters submitting to the instruction to "Stay away from all books. You must first get some lessons in phonics."

Among those who endorse packaged programs—usually beginning with the kindergarten—not all totally agree with the criticism directed against all techniques except phonics. The technique most of them do denounce is that of recognizing words at sight as a picture or a whole unit. This method, they charge, has led many children to fail to learn to read. The fact that many preschoolers have acquired most of their  reading vocabulary in this way, without any "reading lesson," is immaterial to such critics. Many of them also denounce another method of unlocking a word, widely used and strongly endorsed by reading specialists, that of attempting to discover what a given word is through the context. A child who is reading "Jimmie ran to meet his ———," and is blocked by the next word, may pause to think, "Who might Jimmie run to meet?" and supply the word *brother* from recalling previous elements of the context. He may also use pictures as clues to words.

Error 5. Recognition of a word by its appearance or configuration, by context clues, or by picture clues has helped children develop their own resourcefulness and grow more independent in their reading. Yet some producers of phonics systems are vigorous in denouncing the foregoing procedures, claiming that they encourage a child to *guess* what a word is and that guessing is "bad education." These critics might profit from Bruner's statement on the subject of guessing:

Possibly there are certain kinds of situations where guessing is desirable and where it may facilitate the development of intuitive thinking to some reasonable degree. There may, indeed, be a kind of guessing that requires careful cultivation. Yet, in many classes in school, guessing is heavily penalized and is associated somehow with laziness. Certainly one would not like to educate students to do nothing but guess, for guessing should always be followed up by as much verification and confirmation as necessary; but too stringent a penalty on guessing may restrain thinking of any sort and keep it plodding, rather than permitting it to make occasional leaps.[4]

Young children who guess at words are taught to verify later on by asking a teacher or abler reader. Furthermore, they are encouraged to "take note of the word" so they can recall it more readily in the future. The value of such learning is multiple: The child learns to recognize the word, to help himself, to check when in doubt, and to make a mental note of the appearance of the word in some way—depending upon the word and his own uniqueness—thereby reinforcing his remembering techniques.

Fortunately, not all promoters of phonics systems join in wholesale condemnation of children's self-help word-recognition pursuits. In addition, some widely used systems recognize that many words in our language cannot be "sounded out," and, because even beginning readers meet such words as *one, sure,* and *once,* they advocate that these words be taught as sight words. This concession is a help to teachers and, obviously, a boost to children's freedom to learn. Observant teachers report, however, that no matter how emphatic the instructions to follow

---

[4] *Ibid.,* p. 64.

a prescribed method of recognizing words, eager learners will use their own ideas and will employ all word-recognition techniques, thereby resisting the restrictive influences of the least psychologically sound programs. Perhaps only the docile and less aggressive learners are slowed down or thwarted.

Error 6. The gibberish of the old school is almost forgotten. Some of us can recall the long rules we memorized and recited distinctly upon call, but which meant little or even the wrong thing to us, such as "Always remember to dot your *i*'s and cross your *t*'s." Perhaps this is why one so often sees a word in capitals with an *i* dotted. The rule was good as far as it went, but it failed to add "except when writing capitals."

Child psychologists, over a long period of years, have recommended that teachers avoid giving children a rule or generalization to memorize before they have had enough experience to understand its reasonableness. (Exceptions are made in experiences fraught with danger and in emergencies.) Once a child is experienced with words in his reading and has come to notice irregularities—as well as consistencies—he is ready to understand and accept the wisdom of phonics. For a few, this time comes in the first grade; for the majority, in the second; and for more, in the third. When they are older, they are also able to understand and enjoy some of the history of the growth of our language, including the extent of borrowing from other languages and determining the antiquity of some of our spellings. They are also ready for an exploration of a clear-type dictionary and of the variety of aids dictionary authors use to help us pronounce words correctly, such as phonemic spelling and diacritical marks.

Erroneous teaching about phonics. Not only do they hold many mistaken ideas about the learning methods of young children, but some of the designers of phonics theories, methods, and materials make grave errors in the very field that is their specialty—phonics, the sounds of letters and combinations of letters.

Error 1. A widely publicized system introduces children to "sounding out" the alphabet in sequence. It assigns one particular sound to each letter; for example, *a* is pronounced as *ä*, *b* as *bä*, *c* as *kä*, and so forth. As already cited in Chapter 2 of this book, however, the multiple sounds of letters form one of the difficulties a child must overcome if he is to become an independent reader. For example, *a* has eight distinctive sounds listed for it in common dictionaries. The consonant *b* is blended into *bad, bed, big, bone, bloom, bright,* so that it "sounds different" to the child. According to the system referred to, a child first sounds out all the letters in the words, then blends the letters into the proper word. A child who dutifully accepts this formula may have quite a struggle to pronounce *ice* in *ice-cream,* a word he cannot help meeting, or the *a* in a word starting with *fa* that may be *făt* or *fāte.*

From systems that put emphasis on one given sound per letter as a beginning approach, a child quite naturally makes the assumption that learning to sound out words is a reasonable matter of learning to pronounce each letter—the rest is a simple application of that learning. What ignorance of our language or what dishonesty in teaching! Children resent, and rightfully so, being told later on, "Oh, now you are ready to know the whole answer." Sensitive parents and teachers are well aware of this resentment.

Error 2. A second error doubtless arises out of the dilemma of attempting to teach the too-young some of the too-difficult rules plus their exceptions. To meet this problem, the child is gradually introduced to the whole rule. For example, vowel diphthongs as a rule take the long sound of the first vowel. Some words that follow this rule, such as *coat, boat,* and *wait,* are familiar to a child, so this part of the rule can be understood and applied by many. But what about the many exceptions, as in the commonly used *head, read* (past tense), and *heard?* A teacher may say, "This group is not ready to go into the exceptions." Furthermore, many six- and seven-year-olds are not yet able to understand what is meant by the phrases "as a rule" or "in general."

Attempting to proceed with young children in beginning reading on a strictly phonic approach as the sole basis for recognizing words is certain to lead a teacher into difficulty and children into confusion, if not discouragement. Even if only regular words are carefully selected, children's interest, once whetted, will lead them to books, signs, and television script, and thus to many words that are not regular. The children are right if, in dismay, they protest, "My phonics don't work."

Erroneous implications about the reality of reading. The big event for a child entering first grade is learning to read. Most healthy, alert youngsters expect to learn to read on the first day of school, even in a day full of other adventures and real excitement. Many teachers, respecting this eagerness, plan some early simple reading, such as a name card on which is written in clear manuscript, "My name is Roberta," or, "I am Michael." They place memos and essential signs at a child's eye level about the room and call them to the children's attention when the signs are needed. They put books of divergent styles and topics on a library table and talk about words during a story hour.

Error 1. This procedure cannot be followed if certain restrictive phonics programs are used. The instruction in some is to defer use of *all* reading until a certain period of phonics work—six or eight weeks in duration—has been accomplished. A child from a literate background who understands from his own experiences that reading is a process through which he can discover stories, news items, and personal messages may understand this sojourn into letters without words, or words without meaningful settings. He may, therefore, see the connection between this fragmentation and reading. One very active six-year-old, the son of a newspaper writer, arrived at school the second Monday of the fall semester and, with some scorn in his voice, asked the teacher, "Are we going to have more of that phonics stuff today?" But to many, not so verbally experienced, the work on phonic elements may mean *reading*. Six-year-old Gertie, to her aunt's question, "What are you reading in school?" answered, "We read *ab* and *an* and *at*."

Sugar-coating real learning, which often occurred in primary grades years ago, has properly been discouraged. Through it, children were duped into learning essentials but were denied the right to know the quality of their learning. They played games with the "little choo-choo chair" and "swang on the swing with ring, ding, ding." Today, a child may be duped into thinking that sounding out phonic elements is reading. One archdefender of an all-phonic approach claims that children of a certain European country can read everything by the time they enter their second or third year of school. He also says, "Of course, they may not understand what they read, but they can pronounce the words."

Hiding the reality of reading is a colossal deception of children. Even a casual acquaintance with them will reveal their readiness for books and their awareness of the many purposes for which we read. Such enlightenment should not be deflected or "put on ice," even for a few weeks. In the next chapter, some of the ways in which young children acquire knowledge of phonics as they enjoy interesting reading will be described.

Error 2. At the present time, there seems to be a rising controversy about when to start teaching reading to young children. Advertisements have appeared offering methods and materials for teaching toddlers at two the beginnings of reading. There is real pressure on nursery schools and on parents of preschoolers to give their three- and four-year-olds the advantages of an early beginning in reading, not in the normal fashion in which children of this age learn, but rather according to a formulated, structured approach. Movies of children using some of these plans demonstrate that they can learn letters and words as early as two, three, and four years of age. The gross error in this trend is in assuming that what a child *can be taught to do* is *ipso facto* the *desirable* thing for him to do.

Careful studies of premature learning have shown that children tend to slough off such efforts and return to a learning pace normal for them. These studies are disregarded, and there is a lack of evidence of the effect of learning to read before five on such readers once they became eight or ten. Callous recklessness is the only proper term for such manipulation of young children.

Error 3. So loudly and so persistently have critics told the public "Today's children can't read," "Today's children can't read because they have not been taught phonics," "Today's children are failing because they can't read because they were not taught phonics," that—like the German people under the influence of Hitler's big-lie technique—fine, reasonable citizens have become alarmed. And, sorry to say, many such citizens reflect the lacks in their own education when, instead of asking, "What are the evidences?" they appear at school offices and ask, "Why don't you teach phonics so children learn to read?"

Periodically, published reports present the facts about children's reading accomplishments. Various magazines, including professional educational journals, have presented evidence that not only are today's children reading well, but that, in city after city, when tests given decades ago are administered to present-day youngsters, today's children exceed the scores made by school-age children in the earlier years. Not only do they score well, but children today also are recognized library-card carriers, reference-book readers, and book owners. The array of books published annually for children ranging from preschool age on up is staggering in number and exciting and convincing proof of the demand of genuine readers taught in the schools.

In addition to such evidence available for the reading, countless librarians, parents, relatives, teachers, and other school personnel can report on the reading of children whom they know and with whom they work. Yet, in spite of all the facts to support the statement that today's children are active, selective, genuine readers, the unsubstantiated rumors persist. Why?

A deep and pervasive study of the reason for this uproar, with its accompanying recommended solution of a brand of phonics, might reveal some interesting, perhaps startling, underlying causes. One well-known critic had a child who was tense and unhappy. The child could not "let go," become relaxed, and learn to read; and his father blamed the school. Finally, he publicized his criticism, "The schools forbid teachers to teach phonics." Other critics, noting the ready appetite for books that attack the schools, became intrigued with the publicity and the lucrative effects of work with the "Let's Save the Kids' Reading" cause. They added to the uproar.

Undoubtedly, there are other reasons—and some are ethical and professional. Nevertheless, thanks to such pressures, some teachers actually feel guilty when children enjoy library books; some children are denied a happy time in learning to read; and, in some classrooms, senseless high verbalization of phonics rules saps time and vitality that could be devoted to creative, intuitive thinking.

As with all waves of interest—or bandwagons, or panaceas—"this, too, shall pass." But children are of kindergarten or first-grade age only once. Unlike a botched painting that an artist can wash out and recreate, a child's botched first attempts at reading cannot be erased. They may affect his progress for years to come.

The teacher and the new phonics panaceas

Unfortunately, the extravagant claims made for some specific phonics systems and the pressures upon school leaders to "adopt" them often silence further inquiry from teachers. No wonder. One creator of an all-phonics method claims, in selling it to board members and administrators, that "If all teachers use my system properly, all children in first grade will succeed in reading." If a child fails to succeed, the system is not at fault; it is the teacher. A teacher under such duress can scarcely be expected to maintain an inquiring attitude. Some successful, intelligent teachers have resigned from school systems rather than submit children to a narrowing start in reading. The tragedy of bright young readers in such situations, who are actually held back in reading progress, tends to go unnoticed. The children respond "according to demand," so why probe further? The great fiction, "All learn successfully," continues to be used as a selling point.

When school leaders encourage professional growth of their staff members through cooperative planning and decision-making, teachers who are up to date in their knowledge of psychological principles applied to teaching reading discuss the selection or rejection of all methods and materials, including

phonics materials. In such situations, teachers do not have to face the dilemma of abdicating from professional standards in order to "prove" the effectiveness of a phonics panacea or any other panacea. Intelligent teachers are eager to try all promising ways of working with children to guarantee their optimum growth. They are also aware of the wide divergence in children's ways of learning that makes it impossible for any *one* method or any *one* brand of material to fit the educational specifics of all. Children in schools engaging in such careful planning are thereby protected from a succession of teaching fads.

No person with even a casual acquaintance with the spelling of English words and the problems it causes beginning readers minimizes the difficulty of teaching beginners how to read. No such person will ignore the importance of phonics in the total process of becoming a reader. Nor can he believe that the vagaries of English spelling can be taught to a child who has not matured enough to deal with inconsistencies or to manage intellectually adult logical sequences.

The English reading specialist I. J. Pitman has spearheaded a more forthright program than many that have arisen on this side of the Atlantic. He has fostered the use of a 40-sound, 43-character, lower-case roman alphabet for beginners, the Augmented Roman Alphabet. He has also initiated genuine efforts to test its effectiveness. These investigations are to be continued over several years.[5] Several schools in the United States are also experimenting with the Augmented Roman Alphabet. No particular method is prescribed in connection with the use of the revised alphabet, and it is intended for the first years of reading only.

The effectiveness of all proposals must ultimately be measured by the quality of readers taught in accordance with them. A carefully planned evaluation of all such proposals should be undertaken. To do this, the planners should gather the evidences of children's growth in wide and extensive reading of a selective and critical nature and compare these data with those gathered similarly from youngsters taught via the "new era" method. They should carefully examine whether the present emphases on the technical aspects of reading, and on phonics in particular, are valuable enough to warrant limiting and discouraging for beginners the enjoyable use of the full function of reading. On this point, the linguist Charles C. Fries, who has remained deeply interested in the work of the schools, states: "Even from the beginning there must be complete meaning responses not only to words but to complete utterances and, as soon as possible, to sequences of utterances. The cumulative

---

[5] I. J. Pitman, "Learning to Read," *Journal of the Royal Society of Arts.* London, February 1961.

comprehension of the meaning must become so complete that the pupil reader can as he goes along supply those portions of the language signals which the bundles of spelling patterns alone do not represent."[6]

Promising methods and materials are desired, and their developers will welcome a critical test of their worth. Those which are highly publicized but unproven should be avoided as judiciously as heart specialists avoid quackery. One obligation remains—namely, to insure optimum learning of today's children.

---

[6] Charles C. Fries, *Linguistics and Reading*. New York: Holt, Rinehart and Winston, Inc., 1962, 1963, p. xvii.

5. Sensible use of phonics in beginning reading

Children themselves offer one of the most reassuring notes in the controversy over phonics. If they are given half a chance, they survive absurd and phony attempts to control their behavior. A child who has had a wholesome family life in his pre-school years, who looks forward to school, and who has already developed a love of books and of learning will persist in activities that build on this foundation. When he is confronted with some materials and methods that seem peculiar, even sense-less, he may respond amiably, like eight-year-old Steve, who said, "Oh, that's just some of the funny stuff you have to do in school." An important point to keep in mind, however, is that a child can draw upon the "insulation" he received prior to school only as long as he does not receive jolts that harm him basically. For example, if he should become disillusioned with learning and acquire a hate for school, or if he begins to feel unhappy about his own ability to learn, the cause for such deviation should be a matter of concern at home and in school.

Another reassuring observation regarding children that needs to be emphasized and re-emphasized is that they learn in count-less ways. They "latch on" to words, to ideas, and to physical and mental skills. It is impossible to prevent them from learning. A parent who fears that the school is not using the *best method* or *material* can relax. As long as those at home treat the youngster sensibly, he probably will learn to read in school no matter what peculiar methods are used.

Even if children have great personal resources with which to meet inferior school situations, such experiences can dampen their eagerness, retard their rate of learning, and create blind spots. They deserve, therefore, a serious pursuit of the most intelligent way of guiding them. Because every parent and individual teacher has an important role to play in a child's early reading-phonics career, some suggestions are included here as encouragement. Let us hope that no one will follow the decision of the upset mother who made a hand-rinsing gesture and said, "I'm keeping my hands off the whole reading business with Junior. I'm leaving it all up to the school."

Phonics learning in preschool years

A parent, aware of the true value of everyday experiences to youngsters, can plan for them more readily and can derive personal satisfaction through observing a child's reactions. The following suggestions have been tried out in many a home, and they inspire other activities. Some of these suggestions may seem remote from phonics, but they are intended to serve as foundation builders. Participation in the following activities can help a child to enlarge his vocabulary, to amplify the meanings of words, to notice signs, printed instructions, and key letters, and, above all, to become aware of the importance and use of reading in the life around him.

1. *Include a child, whenever feasible, in household work.* Such work could be baking, planting seeds, repairing a toy, washing the car, or the like.

2. *Engage him in conversation while at this work.* Use language essential to the work. Clear, distinct conversation at such times not only helps him to hear a good model of English but also allows his ears to become experienced in hearing it. If he garbles words, make it a point to reuse those words, pronouncing them clearly. Tell older children not to laugh at him or imitate his errors. Include older children in the working-together projects, demonstrating a respect for "each according to his ability."

3. *Keep memos.* A child can acquire a respect for the necessity of such reminders. Ask him to tell you when to write a memo, lest you forget to: "Make some more popsicles," or "Go

to Kathy's house tomorrow." Refer to these memos. At times, run your finger under words from left to right. When he reads part of a memo, stop, listen, and comment favorably. He may reveal to you how much he has taken in by watching you write. He may even want to write a letter or two. One child kept the memos his mother tore from the pad and, to her surprise, learned to read some of the words from them. The writing should be clear; all capitals would be better than lower-case cursive script.

A reminder. You will notice that a child identifies words often before he can identify individual letters. Words are pictures to him. The "logic" of spelling out or sounding out as a beginning approach is denied by the children's ability to recognize whole words even before they recognize letters. Concern for individual letters may not develop until they want to write. (More information on writing will be given later in this chapter.)

4. *Call attention to signs and labels when traveling together.* When a child asks, "What is that word?" tell him. If he has heard older youngsters spell out words and asks you to spell a word for him, do it. This may be a passing interest, but, even if it is, it leaves a residue of increased awareness.

5. *Read together.* Let the child sit close enough to look into the book. Occasionally, run your finger across the lines as you read, going slowly when he seems interested. When he wants to fill out a word or phrase in a familiar story, encourage him to do so. When he says, "I know where it says *Flippity Flop*," have him show you and commend him.

You will notice what specialists have observed, that a child grasps things in his own fashion. He may recognize *Flippity Flop* by some cue that he cannot describe to you, just as he may recognize his name with speed and accuracy.

Interest in words may, at times, be the high point in these reading moments, but the key value in shared reading is the development of a child's love of books, knowledge, taste, and genuine motivation to read by himself ultimately. Perhaps no other experiences add so much to a child's future happiness and success in life-long interests.

6. *Enjoy sounds.* These sounds include rhymes, music, catchy words, and chants. Early "ear training" pays off for life, yet it can become a part of life almost without effort, once it is begun. When ascending stairs, children enjoy chanting in time with their steps, "Up one," "Up two," "Up three," and so on. In responding to a child's call, one can answer, "Here I come, here I come." A child soon picks up this practice and responds similarly.

Mother Goose, Edward Lear, A. A. Milne, Rachel Field, Dorothy Aldis, and others offer delightful ear-pleasing rhythms, nonsense words, and poetry for two-, three-, and four-year-olds.

Many nursery rhymes and stories for children have been set to music and are now available for a child's record library.

Singing games, perhaps the old traditional ones like "Here we go 'round the mulberry bush," stimulate young children of three and four to start to sing, to notice high and low pitch and variations in tempo, and to grow in detecting finer shadings of sound. Without any prompting, children sing along with records they enjoy, with radio and television music, and with sales jingles. A singing child is a happy child, but he is also a growing-in-hearing child. He is building readiness for phonics.

Chanting the ABC's and spelling words aloud with a strong beat seem to intrigue children and stir their imaginations. The skipping-rope chants and jingles of older children have been passed along from generation to generation. Singing in time with swinging has become traditional for younger children—the sing-song quality has a soothing effect upon the child, and he enjoys hearing the familiar. Little Marietta expressed it well when she told the nursery-school teacher who had sung one of her favorite songs, "That makes my ears happy."

Even among young children whose ears have been tested for auditory acuity and found to be normal, marked differences can be noted between individuals. Some, although able to hear, are uneducated in sounds; others are "sound-wise." In most instances, the preschool life at home is responsible for the differences.

7. *Play with alphabet blocks.* This play should be in a manner that a child enjoys and can improvise upon. Some parents, so fearful that they may do the wrong thing with anything that pertains to reading, do not permit their children to become acquainted with alphabet blocks. What a denial to the child! Today there are plastic letters in bagfuls that children can play with in many ways of their own creation. One alert child sang the ABC song, then finally learned to arrange the letters in sequence. He started out knowing five or six letters; he asked repeatedly for help in recognizing the others until he accom-

plished his goal. After arranging the letters several times, with less help each time, he announced, "This time I can do it all by myself." And he did. What a joyful way to learn to identify the capital letters.

A seven-year-old "played store" with a five-year-old sister. "Send me three *A*'s" and "I want an *M*." "This is the wrong letter; it's a *B*, I ordered a *D*." The five-year-old in this normal child's play began to recognize letters. She was also observed looking intently at letters and pronouncing the names of those she identified to herself, *"B," "O," "S."*

8. *Satisfy an early desire to write.* Most youngsters in a home wish to write when they see others do so—imitation is a powerful influence in learning. At first, a youngster may merely wish to use a crayon or pencil, and scribble. Between the ages of four and five, many convey genuine eagerness to write their names or initials. Block play sometimes stimulates children to copy some of the letters. Some pursue such efforts without calling for adult help; others may ask, "Show me how to write my name."

This type of serious request deserves an immediate and helpful response. If the child has already demonstrated that he is right-handed, he should stand at the right side of the writer, close enough to watch as the letters are being written. Slowly and carefully, preferably while describing how to make the letter, a parent or older child may show him: "*N* starts with a straight line from top to bottom, like this. Then I make another line just like it to the right. Then I draw a line from the top of the first line to the bottom of the second line." If you ask a child, "Shall I do it again while you watch?" he will indicate if he is interested.

The reason for placing a child at the right side is to help him establish the proper space relationship in writing. A right-handed person starts from the center of his body and moves out as he writes. A child needs to establish the direction from left, or center, out to the right in both his writing and reading habits. Attention to this at the very beginning prevents confusion later on. A left-handed child may be helped if the parent demonstrating how to write uses his left hand to do so. Such a child will also be less confused when he imitates the writing if he stands at the writer's right side.

Care in showing how to make letters, where to start, and the proper sequence of lines will also help to establish correct writing habits. When children who have not requested help write, it is sensible to observe their method and offer help if faulty procedures are noticed. The size and clarity of letters at the beginning is of minor importance. If children have ample space on their paper and a writing tool that is easy to handle, and if they are unafraid, their writing competence grows and even takes on individuality.

9. *Look for evidences that a child is beginning to read.* Such evidences appear quite frequently with four- and five-year-olds. Interestingly enough, many alert youngsters start via the whole-word approach, the very way in which promoters of some phonics systems say they are prevented from becoming readers. Doubtless, some rely upon interesting letter cues, pictures, and other mechanics in identifying words. Sometimes the cues mislead them. Then they need to be given the right word. For example, four-year-old Jenny saw the word *Jigger* on television and immediately piped out, "There's my name." Her mother said, "It does start with *J* as your name does, but that word is *Jigger*. Your name is *Jenny*. You were right with the first letter."

Between the ages of five and six, alert youngsters develop a continuing interest in reading. They may plague one with the question, "What is this word?" The sensible response is to tell them, pronouncing the word distinctly. Often, they can be heard pronouncing the word over and over half-audibly to themselves—practicing it so that they remember it. Many nimble five-year-olds—and some four-year-olds, too—have taught themselves to read in this simple, informal way. Such a child may enter kindergarten able to read simple stories. But he may become so fascinated by the group life in kindergarten that an early interest in reading fades or, at best, plays a less important role in the child's life during the first half of the year.

Now, the questions so frequently asked by parents: Is this early reading at home good for the child? Will it hamper him in school? Will it confuse him? Unfortunately, there are some teachers, phonics advocates, and reading specialists who do not endorse early reading interests at home. They hold that there is only one way for a child to begin to read—that is, to be taught *via the one method.* Which *one* method varies among those who maintain this position. That children, through their own eagerness and using their own resources, have "taught themselves" to read and have demonstrated successful reading habits is not considered pertinent; neither is there any concern over holding back, or dampening the ambitions of these eager readers.

Other answers to such questions may be given that are based upon long and inclusive observation of such early readers. They are not hampered and will not be confused in school if two common-sense factors are respected:

First, the child should be helped in response to his search for aid, *but he should not be goaded, high-pressured, or forced into beginning reading* by an overly ambitious or misguided parent—or other relative. Such pressures can harm a youngster in more areas than his reading. As a result of too much urging, he may resent the adult, resent reading, and even begin to doubt his acceptability at home. A relaxed, normal parent-child relationship, on the other hand, adds to his sense of closeness to the parent, his joy in learning, and his general feeling of adequacy.

Second, the child profits from before-school knowledge of reading *if he is taught by a sensible teacher,* who respects the vast array of knowledge and skills children reveal upon entrance to school. The teacher who complained to Jack's father, "You've taken the edge off my fun of teaching him because he already knows the alphabet," needs more than a tranquilizer to bring her back to "normalcy." The school leader who sends out instructions to parents of preschoolers, "Don't tamper with their reading. We are educated to look after that," displays a shocking lack of respect for wholesome parent-child relationships, young children's eagerness to learn, and the proper role of the school in meeting individual children with all their strengths and variations.

In all the foregoing suggestions, the key point to keep in mind is to enjoy with the child the exploration of things to see, to listen to, and to engage in. Use a common-sense approach to his questions. Certainly, the free use of books, much enjoyment of reading aloud to him, fun with words, and commenting about letters will fit naturally into such an approach. The result of such fun in life will vary from child to child. Some will become eager, alert, and ready to enter kindergarten and learn with the group under the guidance of a teacher; others, although mildly interested and entertained, will not react pointedly or seem to acquire much.

Phonics in kindergarten

Once a child enters kindergarten, the school part of his daily program rests in the hands of the teacher. The quality of this program may vary from school to school, depending chiefly upon the point of view held toward reading. The main differences center upon two approaches to beginning reading, often referred to as reading-readiness. One approach emphasizes some preplanned method with commercially prepared materials. The other attaches great importance to learning through experiences resembling those of preschool days, but with respect for the added maturity of the children. A brief description of programs with these emphases follows.

Preplanned commercial program. A number of publishers have prepared "pre-reading" or "reading-readiness" types of materials for kindergarten use. Although these materials vary, they tend to include exercises to help children identify letters; to sound letters, usually starting with initial consonants; and to learn to follow instructions with other members in a group. Most are planned to prepare a child for group instruction in a basal reading system used in primary grades. A child who has operated as an individual in preschool years does need to grow in being able to listen to directions intended for him as a group member. The material is carefully prepared and graduated in difficulty. A child's response is controlled; for example, in response to the question, "In what word does *A* come?" he must respond *Apple,* even though he may know a number of words not presented in the material that begin with *A*—such as *About, Alice,* and *Andy.*

Some materials keep the sounding of letters close to the word in which they appear, to avoid the error linguists caution us about, *b* as in *bed,* not *bä-ĕ-dä.* Some, however, advocate the teaching of the "sound of individual letters." The error of such practice is described in Chapter 2.

Simple books are introduced later for those who master the technical elements satisfactorily. The progress within a kindergarten class varies. Some are eager for this type of "lesson" from the first day of school and do well with it; others lag or wander off, appearing to be "not yet ready." Some of these "laggers" may spend another year in kindergarten. The others are usually arranged around tables in groups of six to ten at a set time each day for the next step in the sequence of lessons. Other experiences are engaged upon in the preplanned programs too, but must be limited so that the work of primary importance, reading readiness, is not displaced. This work assumes a uniformity of children's ability, for all are expected to follow the instructions and make the identical responses. A few may attend with interest at first, then become restless and obviously uninterested. They may be too advanced in their reading knowledge to be challenged by the reading-readiness exercises. Unfortunately for such youngsters, a teacher may fail to understand the reason for their boredom and compel them to "pay attention." Some stout resisters to such pressures turn next to disrupting tactics. The undesirable effect of rigid adherence to uniform materials can be observed frequently.

Experience-based program. The experience-based program is quite different. A great variety of materials and things to do makes up the usual order of the day. Emphasis on trips for finding out and discovering, on books for examination and enjoyment, and on children's creative ability to build and construct is kept in the foreground. But attention is paid to the variations in abilities in speaking, listening, illustrating, thinking, and constructing. Those who base their programs on individual differences and readiness for the varied multiple experience that kindergarten can offer reject the early introduction of uniform instruction into the lives of such young children.

Instead, the child's growth in recognizing letters and words, beginnings in phonics and in writing, emerge from and are linked with the interests the children are pursuing. For example, one kindergarten visited a farm in early fall and watched the farmer and his helpers climb ladders to pick apples and then sort them into baskets for the market. Upon their return, several youngsters began to dramatize apple picking. A stepladder was placed near a clothes horse, which had been discovered in a supply room on an early exploratory trip of the school. Then the apple-picking business began. Cartons were salvaged from the cafeteria and, via imagination, filled with apples. The cartons were stacked on a cart and delivered to a hastily improvised store, over which one child insisted a sign, MARKET, be attached. The teacher was asked to make the sign. On a subsequent trip to a supermarket, children noticed how fruit was displayed with price tags. They returned and revived their apple-market play, now adding price tags.

One could feel the burgeoning interest stimulated by the trip to the farm—new language, new meanings, the recognition of the need for signs, and increased alertness. In addition, several of the so-called readier children began to make additional signs, ask for more help in writing, and increase their interest in and knowledge of symbols. Four youngsters began to write their names—and wanted their names placed on more of their in-school "property," such as chairs and lockers.

During the course of a year of such lively getting about and learning, a normal five-year-old acquires a rich background in functional reading and writing. And it all makes sense to him. The approach from a five-year-old's point of view is reasonable. In addition, he has continued to develop his own resourcefulness and creative powers in many skills, as well as in reading. Some, by the end of the kindergarten year, can read simple books, memos, and many signs. They also can write their own names and, often, additional names and common words. Most have learned many of the techniques essential to reading, such as awareness of the left-to-right and top-to-bottom motions in reading and writing. They may recognize and write letters of the alphabet, have a repertoire of stories and experiences in handling books, enjoy listening and retelling stories, and, above all, demonstrate an eagerness to go to first grade and continue learning to read.

A brief evaluation. A child may progress in the specifics of reading in both programs; however, the first one demands that the teacher hamper the child's creative and exploratory ability and perhaps even bore him by expecting him to learn facts he already knows. The second fosters the young child's need to explore by "wiggling his world," yet helps him to gain power in his reading growth. Those who read the pamphlet "A Creative Life for Your Children" by Margaret Mead[1] will appreciate the importance of this approach to children's creative development.

---

[1] Margaret Mead, "A Creative Life for Your Children." Washington, D.C.: U.S. Department of Health, Education, and Welfare, Children's Bureau, 1962 (pamphlet).

The preplanned commercial program encourages a teacher to assume that children's reading needs can be met in groups of "similar" children. The experience-based program is developed on a respect for the uniqueness of each child; none is retarded from reaching higher peaks, and none is dragged beyond his depth and discouraged.

The parents' role. Today's sophisticated parent knows that once a child enters kindergarten, home and "mother" take a second place in his life; school and "my teacher" come first. With normal, unafraid children, the first weeks in kindergarten are highly stimulating, and everything that happens (under a good teacher's guidance) is interesting and worth doing. At this time, the parent should assume an interested but quiet attitude. Once a child lets down and tends to return to "home life as usual," experiences with books, playing familiar games, and going on exploratory trips together will again fit his at-home needs.

Many schools hold a meeting early in the year to describe the nature of the kindergarten program to parents. At this time, they describe their approach to the child's use of symbols. This gives parents an opportunity to learn which type of reading-readiness program is used by the teacher. If such meetings are not sufficiently helpful, interested individual parents can visit school to inquire. It seems highly desirable for parents to understand how a child is being guided in his awareness and use of letters, books, and writing. The parent can then better understand what the child says about his work. Kindergarten children, at best, are not yet able to report many things that a parent is eager to know. Instead, they talk, in spotty fashion, about items that may seem disconnected to us but which are of importance to them. A parent who wishes to be accurately and adequately informed in order to be helpful needs, therefore, to establish a relaxed but informative home-school relationship.

Here are some general guidelines for parents at this time:

1. Speak approvingly to the child of the teacher, the school, and the program—even when in doubt. A child needs to maintain confidence in school, which is now his *business*. If some incidents or practices upset him, assure him you will inquire and that the teacher and you can get matters adjusted. Only if acute upsets that a classroom teacher is unable to alter occur should you seek out the principal or other leader.

2. If a narrow reading-readiness program is used, accept it, and continue to encourage the child's contacts with books and other reading experiences at home "as usual." A child can assimilate boring and prescribed work without being short-changed as long as he is gathering new experience outside school. If, however, he begins to dislike school or does not want to attend, this attitude should be discussed with his teacher.

3. If children ask to continue work at home similar to that at school, make some response so the child does not feel denied or frustrated. Remember, however, that some teachers encourage parents to help them, and others do not. One ingenious parent was asked by young Beth, "Show me a letter and have me tell you what it is—the way the teacher does." The mother responded, "Your teacher does it her way, which I don't know. Let's try it my way." She printed a large *B* plainly on paper and said, "What letter is this?" Beth responded, "That's a *B*. That's not exactly the way my teacher does, she has lots of cards. Make some more, then ask me a lot."

Such requests may be satisfied with momentary help or a few repetitions of the activity, after which a child's interest moves to other things.

4. When some work is brought home, such as an illustration, or a page from a workbook, give this evidence of achievement your wholehearted attention. Rather than asking a child specific questions about it, ask him to "Tell me about it." Some youngsters will give detailed accounts; others may simply toss off, "Oh, it's just something." Further probing may not evoke more from the narrator.

BUT DADDY, HOW CAN YOU BE CERTAIN IT'S *CURTAIN*?

5. If there is concern about programs, make inquiries. A number of parents may be unhappy about "what goes on in kindergarten" or they may disagree among themselves over the kindergarten reading-readiness program. It may be possible to arrange an informal meeting, open to all parents, with the teacher and others whom the teacher considers essential, to enlighten the parents and reduce any concern. One of the more serious problems of such tensions is the inability to keep them from children, thereby affecting the youngsters adversely.

6. If alert youngsters begin to protest and show signs of boredom a few weeks after school has started, investigate. Some may show an unhappiness about school even earlier. It is possible that the school is one of the few which offer static kindergarten programs geared to fit four-year-olds rather than five-year-olds. In such situations, intellectual stimulation may be lacking. A child in a good home and neighborhood situation is often better

off at home than he is in such an unventilated intellectual climate. This should be a matter of concern to the parents of the children. In one school, the parents insisted that a bright young teacher be added to the staff to liven up a program directed by a tired, frail teacher who was due to retire within a few years. In another school, four parents took turns as unpaid aides and added genuine value to the program.

Schools with stimulating in-service programs for the total staff prevent stagnant classroom situations from developing and revive teachers who have tended to weary of their work. In this age of continuing education, a school without a good in-service program is remiss.

7. When a child has already begun to read independently before kindergarten entrance or begins during the year, encourage him. Help him to express his love of books and to increase his reading independence and know-how in a relaxed, matter-of-fact way. Pronounce words for him distinctly, and correct his pronunciation in a clear, friendly way. Be prepared for his interest in reading to wane for long periods at a time.

8. If a child asks for help in writing, find out what type of writing is being taught to him. Most kindergarten teachers use script called "manuscript writing" in writing notes, memos, and key words intended for children. It has now become common practice in many school systems to send a copy of manuscript capital and lower-case letters home as a guide for parents. This is a helpful practice and should be encouraged. But there are still some schools admonishing parents, "Don't help him write at home. You'll confuse him." In such a situation, your request for copies of manuscript and for suggestions may improve this retarded attitude.

How much phonics to expect. In today's uneasy climate, it is only natural for some parents to ask, "Shouldn't kindergarten programs be responsible for teaching beginnings in phonics?"

A stimulating program does—some children progress so far that they can pronounce, via use of phonics, a large number of regular words. They may also recognize many words at sight, some as complicated as *gymnasium* and *congratulations*. Some children, via a commercial system, may not be as mature and independent, but they will have progressed satisfactorily according to the standards set by the system. Less mature ones may have barely inched along or may show no sign of alertness to sounds of words. They may, however, blossom forth during the following summer—or early in first grade.

Tests of a general reading-readiness nature and specific ones for given phonics systems are in use. Specialists in testing and measurement and in kindergarten education, however, call attention to the unreliability of scores based on group tests of such young children. Only a highly competent person, working with each child individually, can arrive at a more reliable score —under ultra-favorable conditions.

An observant teacher and parent can notice and keep a record of evidence of growth in the specifics of phonics. Often a youngster will enter kindergarten quite eager to read and to identify letters and some words. Then, becoming stimulated by learning many things that do not pertain to reading during the year, he may lose much of his interest in phonics and all reading mechanics. Such youngsters, as a rule, again blossom forth in first grade.

These suggestions, to return to a point made at the beginning of this section, may seem remotely connected with phonics. Yet they build foundations for future success not merely in phonics, but in the development of competence in reading. It is well, too, to remind parents and teachers that there is no one, set time when a child is ripe for making beginnings in reading. As long as the adults and children who are important to him do not grow uneasy and show their concern to him, he will capture, or recapture, his reading interest and launch forth in the first grade.

Growth in phonics in first grade

When a child enters the first grade, he and others around him believe that learning to read will be the biggest achievement of the year. Normal, healthy children can expect this to be true—with the help of many methods and great varieties of materials. Unfortunately, many of these beginners will enter schools that, according to current standards, offer a climate just a bit above the minimum literacy level. Such schools maintain no library, provide no books other than basic texts, and supply no professional library for teachers. In these schools, youngsters acquire the mechanics of reading, but few may acquire the zest for reading in continuing everyday life. Nevertheless, some of these schools would meet the approval of several of today's critics, so blinded by word recognition via phonics that they cannot see the sparkling appeal of a life filled with books, newspapers, and current materials. Fortunately for the majority of today's first-graders, the schools they attend offer a challenging reading climate, one that inspires and helps a child continue to learn to read. In these schools, a part of the appeal and motivation to read comes from the availability of books.

Continuing the challenge to read. Approximately 75 per cent to 80 per cent of the six-year-olds who enter first grade become readers during the year. Some, as described before, bring considerable knowledge about reading with them; some already are readers. In any normal situation, several children—at times as many as one-fourth of the class—will struggle along slowly and fall short of first-grade expectations. Some of the less agile ones may be so labeled by inadequate tests. Such youngsters may read and have fine attitudes toward reading and good methods of approaching reading, but the tests may not reveal their ability. An observant teacher and parent, fortunately, can correct the erroneous rating given by such a test.

The methods and materials used in this beginning-reading period vary beyond those described in Chapter 4, yet some common elements in reading programs in schools across the country have been found so helpful that they are included here. They are selected from those that reveal inclusive goals in teaching reading. The hoped-for result of such programs is a child who:

1. Regardless of his ability, enjoys looking at books and listening to stories, news items, and information.

2. Grows in his independent use of reading through recognizing words via phonics, total configuration, letter cues, and structure.

3. Increases in ability to select materials suitable to his need.

4. Demonstrates an increasing depth of understanding.

5. Develops taste—personal preferences—in his continuing pursuit of reading.

The teaching of phonics, in a program of this breadth, is absolutely essential. To concentrate on phonics, however, even for a period of six to eight weeks, to the exclusion of the continued challenge of reading for enjoyment is unpalatable educational fare. Such procedure forces a child to dedicate himself to the narrow success of learning word elements, words out of context, and rules, rather than to experience the excitement and rewards to be gained from the whole process of reading.

Required or "adopted" systems. Many teachers in first grades use prescribed basal materials with suggestions for teaching phonics and one of the all-phonics programs. Many schools that adopt such materials encourage the teacher to use them "with those children who will be helped" and to supplement them with other creative ideas and materials. In such schools, children who have grown past the need for such first-grade work are not held back, and those who seem to go unchallenged are not dragged along.

In other schools, authorities demand, regardless of the wide divergence of reading progress among children, a daily dose or a "uniform lesson," and the teacher must comply. A parent whose child attends one of these schools may need to keep the child's reading interest whetted. He can do so by reading books that the child enjoys and by continuing to help the child recognize words, letters, and printed material of special appeal. It may be necessary to encourage the child to "do your best in school" even if the work seems "too hard *now*." The parent's important role is that of keeping the child's interest in school active and the spark of reading interest glowing. Once extinguished, these qualities may not be rekindled without several years of wise, encouraging, individual guidance.

Teachers, too, even if caught in a prescribed program, can take short moments to stimulate alert children to examine new books and to notice interesting words. It may also be possible to give them specific help in phonics beyond the required content. For example, one teacher was required to use a system that introduced children to phonics through recognition of the long sound of the vowels in such words as *āble, ēat,* and *ōver*. She found several mature six-year-olds rhyming words—*ink, sink, mink*. She wrote these on the board and suggested that whenever they found another *ink* word she would add it to the list. These youngsters were beyond the first lessons in the system, were having fun experimenting with rhyming words, and were extending their knowledge of phonics as well.

Unfortunately, not all teachers extend their efforts in teaching in this way. As recent research[2] in the teaching of reading

---

[2] Mary C. Austin and Coleman Morrison, *The Harvard Report on Reading in Elementary Schools*. New York: The Macmillan Company, 1963.

indicates, some teachers follow a basal system or other program and put forth no effort to meet the variations in ability. At times, they may even have an entire class work on an identical page and give identical responses. Such unenlightened teaching reveals lack of professional leadership and of in-service teacher education, or poor preparation for teaching. *Good school leadership* helps teachers to understand effective ways of meeting more nearly the ability of each child.

Help with specifics. The variations in children's acuteness in sensing sound and in making the connection between sound and letters were described in Chapter 2. An observant first-grade teacher notices which children are quick and which are slow or less experienced in detecting sounds and in associating sounds with symbols. For the latter, more opportunity to listen and to repeat the words and short comments they hear is essential. It is precisely at this point that some beginners meet their biggest learning hurdle.

An inquiring teacher conducted the following informal experiment early in the fall. She had pointed out to the entire group that some words are the same, except for the beginning letter. She wrote *and* on a white chart, large enough for all to see. Then she wrote *sand* and asked how many could read that word. Many could. She then added *hand, band,* and *land.* Some youngsters could identify each word. Some could not. She then showed them six sets of cards that she had made with the *and* words. Each child would have an opportunity to use a set with his teammates and to practice recognizing and pronouncing the words. She could test each one orally on his progress. In her follow-up, she found that more than half could read the four words rapidly without error. Of the remainder, about half could read them with some hesitation and pondering. The rest demonstrated no real awareness of initial consonant; some made no response, and one blurted out one word, "candy."

Obviously, if similar amounts and types of help on any element are given to the total group, no challenge is offered to some children, and others find the work too difficult. The child who is slow to react may need much more personal and detailed help. He may not be intellectually ready yet for an experience with words presented as words, out of a setting meaningful for him. Goading and pressing such a child may frighten him away from reading. Including him with others who are more agile with language while listening to stories, talking about events, and having fun with words will help him to grow in listening, in hearing more acutely, and in catching on to elements of reading. Denying him such experiences or "holding off until he's ready" may keep him from the very stimulation to growth that he needs.

Selection of what to teach. Common questions asked by teachers who are free to guide a group's steps in the use of phonics are "Where do I begin?" and "Is there a proper sequence to follow?" The use of phonics as described in Chapter 3 demands that a teacher understand consonants, vowels, and combinations of consonants and vowels with all their sound variations. In general, initial consonants, such as *m, b,* and *d,* seem easy starting points with many children. However, key names and exciting words stimulate the beginning of interest in phonics for many youngsters. Charles's first association between letters and sound was *ch.* Ellen enjoyed singing out *el, el, el* after hearing her name called. The *z* in *zigzag* sparked the interest of a group of youngsters because one boy observed that his loose front tooth wiggled when he said "zigzag." An observant teacher follows such personal learnings as far as time permits. A parent, too, after noticing a child make an important connection between letters and sounds, can comment favorably in a matter-of-fact way so that the child will be more sure to remember.

Through games with families of regular words selected for

the purpose, long and short vowel sounds and prefixes and suffixes can be introduced. Once a child has met a number of regular words like *made, take, bake, like,* the rule of the long sound of the vowel followed by the silent *e* can be called to his attention, and he can check to see the degree to which this rule applies. Learning such generalizations is appropriate for seven- and eight-year-olds who are over the initial phonic hurdle and are entering spelling and writing activities with increased eagerness and competence.

A practice commonly used by teachers helps beginners sound out words with increased skill. The word is written clearly on a chart with a flo-pen and then talked about. Children are asked to notice interesting elements, letters they like, parts that are familiar, the length of the word, and whether it is tall or flat. During this discussion, the word is mentioned often. In one first grade, the teacher pointed out some long or *big* words the children used. These words were written on the board so the class could count the letters. Long words were called "ten-dollar words." One such word was *dungaree.* The teacher first wrote it, then wrote it below divided into syllables. So stimulating was this new idea of syllables to these first-graders that they began to hunt for longer words, eager to find out from the teacher how many syllables the words contained.

After a word had been examined and talked about, it was carefully written on a chart as a help for remembering. Through such interest in words, examining their makeup and recalling them day after day, these children grew rapidly in recognition of words and ability in pronunciation. The interest was carried over into the exercises in phonics suggested in a teacher's manual of a basal reading system.

An important quality in this teacher's work was that she stimulated great interest in words that *fascinated* the children. They retained this interest when they approached other phonic work. Present-day emphasis on *the right way* and *the right sequence* denies such essential motivation and makes learning

more impersonal and difficult, and therefore less successful.

If a child arrives at the end of first grade with a continuing eagerness to read and with the dogged determination to get help when needed, at home as well as at school, he is on the way to mastery of the phonics needed for successful reading. The more complicated, involved, and irregular elements essential for continuing growth he will learn readily as he continues his study of reading in later grades. He will also be helped, necessarily, as he progresses in spelling and writing.

A home and school climate unruffled by the present agitation over phonics will offer a child the type of help and assurance he needs to maintain sure, steady growth. The child needs to see the main functions of reading all around him in his home and school life. The methods and materials used to help him learn should be so reasonable that they make sense to him. Teaching phonics in isolation from reading and emphasizing it as if it were a magician's potion puts an unnecessary block in a child's path. As Fries writes: ". . . simply to respond to graphic signs by uttering certain sounds is not 'reading.' . . . 'Word calling' (word-pronouncing) without the meaning responses of the patterns that make the language signals of a code is neither reading nor talking."[3]

---

[3] Charles C. Fries, *Linguistics and Reading*. New York: Holt, Rinehart and Winston, Inc., 1962, 1963, pp. 110–20.

6. Postscript on spelling

In reading, a child looks at a collection of letters that forms a word and uses phonics and other skills to pronounce it. In spelling, he hears or "thinks" a word and then uses phonics from memory to spell the word orally if called upon or to write it. To a careless glance, these two functions may appear to be the same. The processes involved, however, are very different. Most of us know avid adult readers, accurate in their recall of ideas that they have read and versatile in the use of a descriptive vocabulary, who admit that they cannot spell. Some of them toss in the added point, "When I was in school, I was an *A* speller." One gifted writer told, amusingly, how he "forgot how to spell" but "loved to recite the rules, like When *y* at the end of a word is preceded by a consonant before adding a suffix beginning with *i* change the *y* to *i* then add the suffix. See? Hot stuff—but I don't use it when I write."

Fortunately for many of us, our spelling is a private affair. We may greet people with "Why so lugubrious today?" without being able to spell *lugubrious*. Unfortunately, many hours in childhood education were devoted to learning good spelling. Still, some of those whose work demands spelling accuracy—secretaries, proofreaders, and so forth—deplore their inaccuracies. Special classes in spelling are offered for adults in response to frequent and urgent requests for help. Some critics hastily and erroneously lump reading and spelling deficiencies into one package and attribute the problems—as they profess to see them—to one cause, namely, lack of proper teaching of phonics in the primary grades. This instant mass-diagnosis is as erroneous when applied to spelling at it is when directed at reading. A brief look at learning to spell will reveal the many possible reasons for spelling difficulties.

Profile of a beginning speller

Preschool youngsters begin to sense spelling procedure in family experiences. "How do you spell *almost?*" asks an eight-year-old of his mother as he writes. A mother may ask, "Daddy, spell *convenience* for me." Chanting *b-i-g, b-i-g, b-i-g,* or similar words is often an accompaniment to swinging and other rhythmic activities. Some parents say, in happy fashion, as they start off to school with a young child, "O.K., let's *g-o,* go." Many five-year-olds start to write their names and a few words independently in kindergarten. For most, however, writing—which makes a child focus on spelling—starts in first grade.

A beginner has to master two difficulties. He must learn specifically what a letter looks like and which way to start and make each part, and he must learn to control his muscles so that the pencil, chalk, or crayon reproduces a close facsimile of the desired letter. In most up-to-date schools, kindergarten children are given occasional help in spelling names and words they are eager to write, but regular work in spelling is deferred until writing ease has been developed. This is not usually accomplished until second grade. Help with such specifics as letter forms and spacing continues even into the upper grades, but a child's all-absorbing effort to write ordinarily relaxes by the time he is eight or nine. Then he can give more attention to spelling.

Motivation to spell. A healthy young child thrives on evidence that he can do things well without adult assistance. Such motivation carries the beginning reader over many of the difficulties of learning to read. So, too, with spelling. At times, however, the unique function of spelling adds to his zest. When reading, a child is deciphering meanings open to anyone; when writing, only he knows what he wishes to communicate. "I wrote my mother a note and nobody dare read it except my mother," announced Gertie, who was described by her teacher as "very sociable but not so hot academically." Nevertheless, she sensed the element of privacy in writing. To be kept private, however, writing demands some degree of independence in spelling.

In first grade, seasonal events and home-school relations stimulate desires to write and also determine the selection of words. In a first grade visited in October, the teacher kept words children wished to write in columns clearly written on a special bulletin board. Some children referred to the lists and needed no further help. Others needed additional help, such as watching the teacher write a particular word on paper near enough to the child so that he could see and *feel* the process. Children who are interested practice by writing words or short-short letters over and over again. An important corollary, which a good teacher knows well, is that a strong desire to write independently will also encourage the desire to spell correctly.

General practices in teaching spelling

As in teaching phonics, many divergent practices are used in teaching spelling, but there are some points of widespread agreement, too. These include:

1. The words taught should be those commonly used by the

child in his speaking. We all tend to draw upon our speaking vocabulary when we write. We need to learn to spell the words we write.

2. A multiple sensory approach is better than emphasis on one sense only; "See the word, spell it to yourself, then write it," or "Say the word to yourself. Then spell it." Eyes, mental images, and ears are essential to a speller, as is the muscular control essential to clear writing.

3. Children show wide variations in spelling facility and show individual variations in the procedures upon which they rely.

4. Clear and correct enunciation is an aid to spelling. A child who says, "I'm inerested," will spell the word interest *inerest*. (A teacher's speech, too, exerts a real influence on children's speech and spelling.)

5. The desire to be a good speller must persist from year to year. Interest in words and in the English language is developed in a good school program. Knowledge about words, which begets greater interest in spelling, also encourages a child's desire to be a good speller.

6. An overemphasis on phonics can produce a poor speller, according to some research. A cursory examination of pages in the child's dictionary will reveal that fewer than 50 per cent of the words are spelled as they are phonetically re-spelled in the dictionary—*center-senter; might-mīt; raise-rāz.*

7. Only rules with wide application are worth learning, and they should be taught *after* a child is acquainted, in reading and speaking, with a number of words to which the rule applies. Such a rule is: "A word of one syllable ending with a single consonant preceded by a single vowel *usually* doubles the final consonant when a suffix is added, as in *let–letting*, and *bat–batter*."

8. Practice, combined with a desire to keep high spelling accuracy, is imperative. At this point, more research is needed. There are able students in the field of spelling who suspect that

limited experiences in writing, and, consequently, limited use of spelling, result in forgetting words previously spelled correctly. Studies might reveal which of the senses is the strongest influence in early learning and in later recall.

Phonics' function in spelling. Although many words in English are not consistent in sound-symbol relationship, phonics is relied upon in spelling along with other knowledge by well-taught children and adults. Long words are broken into syllables and spelled syllable after syllable. Rules are applied as required, as in writing *cat-e-go-ries* and *un-men-tion-able.* The way in which a child spells often offers a clue to his knowledge of phonics and of word structure. For example, when Andy, in his book report, wrote that he had read the entire book, even "the prephase," the teacher knew he meant *preface.* She also guessed that he did not unravel the meaning of "*pre*face."

To beginners, words presented in families are a delight. These young spellers can write quickly and spell accurately a family like *can, man, tan,* and *ran.* With proper teaching from third grade on, they acquire a few rules and increase their progress in independence, often sensing when to apply an all-phonic approach to the spelling, when to rely on memory, and when to seek help.

Skill in spelling, according to large-scale test scores, has declined in recent years, the only skill to show such results. It is also a skill in which a very rapid increase in measurable ability can be accomplished. In a reasonable home and school environment, with proper challenges to stir interest, and with materials that he can use independently, a child can improve and measure his own progress. Some youngsters, as with phonics, seem to meet insurmountable difficulties in learning to spell. If their problem is linked with difficulty in word recognition, especially in applying phonics, the help of a competent specialist is necessary. Children with hearing difficulty, naturally, may carry their inaccurate hearing over into their spelling.

Proof of independence—the use of the dictionary. We adults use a dictionary to check on the meaning of words new to us and on the accuracy of our pronunciation. We frequently turn to a dictionary for help in spelling. For adults, this is considered normal behavior. With proper guidance, such conduct becomes normal for children, too, and at an early age. Seven-year-olds in the second grade can quickly learn to locate many words from their sounds, as one not-so-agile reader demonstrated in looking up the spelling of *veterinary* for the teacher. In this situation, the teacher was writing a story on a chart as the children related it. When one child said, "We called a veterinary," the teacher started to write, but stopped after *vet* and said, "I don't know how to spell *veterinary.*" Quickly, one boy took a dictionary from the shelf and, with a determined air, located the correct page, and exclaimed—pointing—"I found it." He then spelled it orally for the teacher. "How did you know it was *veterinary?*" asked the teacher. "Because it started with *vet* and was a long word." This boy—a seven-year-old—was not one of the agile readers, yet his ability to help himself revealed genuine resourcefulness. Clear-type dictionaries for this age are available, and using them adds to children's feelings of importance, gives them overt evidence that they are growing up, and encourages their interest in the meaning and spelling of words.

The answer to the entire phonics problem

One ten-year-old boy, who had mediocre achievement in all the skills but was noted for his curiosity, his interest in science experiments, and his knack for asking probing questions, came to school following the mid-year holidays with a "new look." He had been given a dictionary for Christmas, and he was already acquainted with it and rather adept in its use. He was particularly anxious to report a discovery to the whole class, once it was assembled and ready to listen. The discovery he reported was: "Look, you know how much trouble we have in learning to spell straight, and in learning to pronounce new words in our reading too. Well! In this book any word that is spelled silly is first spelled silly. Then after that it is spelled exactly the way it sounds. I tried myself and I could spell any word that way. So— why don't we let the dictionary people print everything for us not the silly way but their way. And we will copy their spelling when we write."

Until this day, for which G.B.S., too, yearned, a commonsense approach and sensible use of facts about children, their ways of learning, and the English language will be the safest course upon which to rely.

Helpful references for wider reading

CARROLL, JOHN B. *The Study of Language.* Cambridge: Harvard University Press, 1952.

DURKIN, DOLORES. *Phonics and the Teaching of Reading.* New York: Bureau of Publications, Teachers College, Columbia University, 1962.

FRIES, CHARLES C. *Linguistics and Reading.* New York: Holt, Rinehart and Winston, Inc., 1962, 1963.

GANS, ROMA. *Common Sense in Teaching Reading.* Indianapolis and New York: The Bobbs-Merrill Company, Inc., 1963.

LANDRETH, CATHERINE. *The Psychology of Early Childhood.* New York: Alfred A. Knopf, 1960.

MCKIM, MARGARET G. *Guiding Growth in Reading.* New York: The Macmillan Company, 1955.

SPACHE, GEORGE D. *Toward Better Reading.* Champaign, Illinois: Garrard Publishing Company, 1963.

STRICKLAND, RUTH. *The Language Arts.* 2nd ed. Boston: D. C. Heath and Company, 1957.

Index

Abbott, Allan, 14
Ability, 28, 38–39, 44, 49, 53, 69, 78, 87, 99
Accent, 17, 22, 25–26
Accuracy, 71
Adequacy, 76
"Adopted" systems, 87–89
Aggressiveness, 38, 56
Aldis, Dorothy, 71
Alertness, 53, 59
Alphabet, 20, 53, 57, 65, 76, 79
Alphabet blocks, 72–73
"Anti-Progressive education," 14
Anxiety, 3, 15, 83
Articulation, 35–36
Artley, A. Steryl, 47
Assimilation, 39–41
Assurance, 43
Attention, 40, 78, 82
Audiometer test (*See* Tests)
Auditory acuity, 33, 49, 72
   (*See also* Hearing)
Augmented Roman Alphabet, 65
Austin, Mary C., 88*n.*

Barnhart, Clarence L., 47
Basal reading system, 77, 89, 91
Basic texts, 86
Behavior, 31, 42, 99
Betts, Emmett, 47

Biology, 31
Bloomfield, Leonard, 47
Books, 36–38, 49–50, 58–60, 62, 71, 77, 79, 81–82, 84, 86
   love of, 67
Boredom, 82
"Brand" systems, 46
Bruner, Jerome S., 51*n.*, 55
Bulletin boards, 96

Capitals, 70, 73, 84
Carroll, John B., 46, 101
"Catchy" titles, 47, 71
Chanting, 71
Chase, Stuart, 44
Child psychologists, 56
Children
   assumptions about, 29–30, 48–56
   differences between, 30–33
   guidance of, 44–45
   individual learning power of, 38–39, 89–90
   influence of environment on, 32–38
   kindergarten, 76–86
   labeling of, 33
   methods of learning of, 39–44
   older, 52, 56
   preschool, 68–76